CU00793472

HowExpert Presents

Forensic Psychology 101

A Quick Guide That Teaches You the Top Key Lessons About Forensic Psychology from A to Z

HowExpert with Sharlaine Ortiz

For more tips related to this topic, visit HowExpert.com/forensic.

Recommended Resources

- HowExpert.com – Quick 'How To' Guides on All Topics by Everyday Experts.
- HowExpert.com/books – HowExpert Books
- HowExpert.com/products – HowExpert Products
- HowExpert.com/courses – HowExpert Courses
- HowExpert.com/clothing – HowExpert Clothing
- HowExpert.com/membership – Learn All Topics from A to Z by Real Experts.
- HowExpert.com/affiliates – HowExpert Affiliate Program
- HowExpert.com/jobs – HowExpert Jobs
- HowExpert.com/writers – Write About Your #1 Passion/Knowledge/Expertise.
- YouTube.com/HowExpert – Subscribe to HowExpert YouTube.
- Instagram.com/HowExpert – Follow HowExpert on Instagram.
- Facebook.com/HowExpert – Follow HowExpert on Facebook.

3

Table of Contents

Chapter 1: Foundations

Psychology and the Legal Field

The need for the intersect between legal matters and the field of psychology was perhaps evidenced through the birth of forensic psychology. This cross-disciplinary approach could be considered to be the use of psychological research, theories, practice, and treatment over a legal setting (González-Sala et al., 2017). Additionally, the application of the scientific foundations of psychology in civil and criminal settings also provided the development of new techniques and procedures to particularly cater to the forensic field (González-Sala et al., 2017). Some observations and studies that seeded the relevance of psychology in this legal arena stem from contributions regarding the use of witnesses and testimonies. Over a century ago, Wilhelm Stern provided insights as to the implications of memory relating to a witness' account, as well as practitioners becoming expert witnesses (Shaw, Öhman, & van Koppen, 2013).

Court System Elements

The court system includes a wide range of professionals that are instrumental in both specific stages and throughout the proceedings. Several elements could be explored as means to provide a focus to its pertinent structures in the United States. The first aspect to consider is the federal nature of judicial processes. In this case, the central government of the nation carries the powers that the incorporated states cannot execute as inherent sovereignty (Melton, Petrila, Poythress & Slobogin, 2007). Therefore, the federal government receives its governance from the Senate and the House of Representatives; and it is modulated by the Supreme Court Justices (Melton et al., 2007). Consequently, this element impacts district court cases at the federal level, thus consisting of a superseding hierarchy when accounting for local and state law. The second element to consider is criminal adjudicative processes. As it relates to the federal district courts, an individual could be prosecuted given an alleged violation of the law that could result in criminal punishment (Melton et al., 2007). In this regard, the prosecuting attorneys could be entrusted, by the federal government, to address which criminal offenses might be presented against a defendant (Melton et al., 2007).

Element Relationship

The relationship between forensic psychology and each of the previous elements of the court system could be conceptualized under a practitioner's roles. For instance, cases presented in district courts at the federal level could make use of forensic practitioners as evaluators. Here, the defense could request forensic practitioners to determine which, if any, mental health issues could have directly impacted the offense at hand (Melton et al., 2007). This process could be part of a possible plea such as that of "not guilty because of insanity" ([NGRI]; Melton et al., 2007). In this case, a practitioner could make use of medical, historical, criminal (Bonnie & Slobogin, 1980), and assessment data as means to assist the judicial process in ascertaining if an NGRI resolution is warranted. This type of defense can later be contested by the prosecution (Bonnie & Slobogin, 1980), which could result in yet another role for the practitioner in the criminal process. A forensic psychologist could be summoned as an expert witness. This type of role could be commonly found in criminal proceedings as recommended by both the defense and the prosecution (Bonnie & Slobogin, 1980). While executing this role, expert witnesses could expect that prosecuting attorneys scrutinize their opinions as means to favor a potential conviction (Babitsky & Mangraviti, 2000). Working as an expert witness in a district court along with the prosecution might be appealing for several professional reasons. However, such role in this setting implies a great familiarization with higher order laws that might not generally be sought after in everyday practice. Further, the challenges that the expert role entails provide forensic practitioners with an ever-changing and complex arena.

Psychology and Legal System

Given the array of sub-specialties in general psychology, it is imperative to analyze how this field has contributed to branches outside the mental health setting. This is the case of general psychology as it is applied to the legal system. Some scholars argue that such application of psychology remains a topic of debate when considering its definition as a *forensic* concept. Some contend that applying general psychology concepts in a legal context inherently develops an intersection known as forensic psychology (Huss, 2001). Yet, other scholars argue that forensic psychology is not the sole application of general psychology knowledge, but rather, it might refer to clinical practitioners executing their roles in a legal setting. Whether considering general or clinical applications, this can be identified in two areas: research and consultation in civil and criminal settings.

Forensic Psychology Benchmarks

Overview

Despite its relatively recent development, it could be argued that forensic psychology has become a significant part of multiple areas. These influences have promoted the development of research and application for psychological practitioners and the interest of laypersons. This subfield's term was coined from judicial processes that took place in ancient Roman forums where dispute defenses occurred (Huss, 2001). In a similar fashion, forensic psychology could be broadly considered as the application of clinical knowledge in a legal setting (Huss, 2001). However, it is relevant to consider how psychological research and practice was ultimately applied in a law environment. One significant aspect of forensic psychology history is its potential origins. Researchers suggest that James McKeen Cattell provided initial insights regarding testimonies during the second half of the 19th century (Bartol & Bartol, 2012). Here, Cattell made use of a student sample, where each was inquired to describe the weather conditions of that past week (Bartol & Bartol, 2012). The testimonies of the students varied drastically from one statement to the next (Bartol & Bartol, 2012), notwithstanding the apparent simplicity and recent occurrence of events. A second significant aspect of forensic psychology benchmarks is its recent recognition as a particular subfield of psychology in the United States; with origins tracing back to the late 20th century.

Evolving of the Field

These historical benchmarks have provided significant contributions to the evolving field of forensic psychology. For instance, vast contributions have been provided when considering the capabilities to testify in a court of law. This topic of interest is currently studied in forensic research and applied during competency, individual selection, and witness evaluation by expert practitioners. One could argue that Cattell's rudimentary experiment provided a foundation for the present-day psychology applications in legal contexts. Concerning the historical recognition of forensic psychology as a sub-field, the intermingling of psychological fields should be considered. Currently, the inclusions of other areas such as developmental, social, and clinical fields are not only included in forensic psychology guidelines but are recognized as instrumental parts of its future (American Psychological Association, 2016b). The original application of general psychological concepts is currently emplaced in forensic psychology but has evolved into an integrative approach with other fields and their contributions in legal arenas.

Contribution Impact

First, psychological research might significantly affect the legal setting by attempting to understand human behavior before its presentation in a legal context. For example, research might provide insights into how a person's lifespan development, personality, and risk factors might impact criminal behavior and its potential re-occurrence. The second application is the psychologist's consultation in a forensic context. This consultation can take the form of a psychologist conducting a clinical assessment (Huss, 2001) or as an expert witness (Bartol & Bartol, 2012) amongst others. For instance, a psychologist might provide an informed assessment of a relevant psychological illness (Huss, 2001) that affected the individual's ability to comprehend the civil or criminal accusation (Bartol & Bartol, 2012). Furthermore, psychological practitioners could provide expert testimony as means to determine potential future violent behavior (Huss, 2001).

Consultation

Overview

The consultation of forensic psychology professionals is arguably as varied as the interests of its practitioners. Likewise, the need for specific forms of consultation also provides a highly diverse focus for consultation. Consequently, let us consider two forms practitioners could consider within areas of forensic psychology consultation. The first type of consultation is records and transcript review. As this term implies, a legal party requests the services of the practitioner as means to conduct a review of multiple data sources (McKee, n.d.). In this case, historical documents could be part of the review to include previous medical and psychological reports (McKee, n.d.). Further, legal documents such as transcripts and statements could be part of the record review (McKee, n.d.). It must be noted that this form of consultation does not include direct contact with examinees, but rather, records that might be part of their case (McKee, n.d.). Another form of consultation involves a specific type of work and population: the potential rehabilitation of juvenile defendants. The particular concept of the recognition of a separate type of court for juveniles originated from the pretense of their rehabilitation over punishment (Gottlieb & Coleman, 2012). In this regard, forensic practitioners could be asked to address the potentiality of treatment as it relates to a particular crime as conducted by the juvenile offender (Melton, Petrila, Poythress, & Slobogin, 2007).

Consultation Challenges

Despite that these two forms of consultation spark some interest due to previous record analysis familiarity and target population, such duty might still present some challenges. For example, one difficulty concerning the area of forensic psychology consultation records and transcript review revolves around possible ethical concerns. It could be argued that inexperience might elicit faulty or far-fetched conclusions that extend beyond the scope of the documents at hand. On the same token, an inexperienced forensic psychology consultant might fail to recognize emerging issues of a record review. These other areas of examination could include recognition signs of the defendant's limited ability in regards to their competency to confess (McKee, n.d.). Careful record analysis and cross-referencing with collateral information, such as pretrial document review (Moses, 2001), could be used to limit such deficiencies. A specific concern regarding juveniles is the enhanced possibility of an examinee "faking good" or "faking bad" as it relates to symptoms (Melton et al., 2007) that could affect treatment recommendations. To minimize the impact of this challenge, consultants should make use of instruments that specifically cater to this population while incorporating scales or instruments of malingering.

Consultation Breakdown

Given a variety of factors, perhaps due to experience or ingenuousness, individuals who wish to become forensic psychology practitioners could be drawn to specific areas of consultation. For example, an area of forensic psychology consultation of interest is the two techniques of interviewing and interrogation. These law enforcement-centered procedures involve the utilization of attempting to discern which statement might be false and later facilitate obtainment of confessions, respectively (Kassin et al., 2010). As such, it is appealing to study, evaluate, and analyze such processes; not from the viewpoint of an interviewer, but rather as a consultant. The second area of interest involves the area of jury selection. This aspect consists of the elimination of individuals that might not be deemed fit to possibly execute a verdict in a specific case (Hutson, 2007). This consultation subject field is appealing given a variety of reasons. First, jury selection methods of elimination could spark the appeal of aspiring forensic professionals as it is a form of forensic practice where the examinees are not facing trial, but rather potentially imparting a trial themselves. It could be argued that many commonly attributed methods of consultation revolve around the stereotypical assumption that practitioners most often address defendants. Lastly, addressing other individuals performing civil duties might also translate into an underlying civil duty service at the end by the practitioner.

Jury Selection

There are civil and criminal court cases that might be resolved with the sole involvement of legal professionals. Yet, there are other instances that laypersons might be called upon to address the verdicts of the remaining cases. This need then calls for the inclusion of a jury of the defendant's peers (Hutson, 2007). Jury selection is the process used which discerns among individuals that are the fittest to address a specific case.

As it could be derived given the myriad of factors that should be accounted for in this process, multiple resources should be explored. Forming forensic psychology practitioners could be encouraged to make use of means to become knowledgeable and skilled in this area. For example, one historical piece of resource to consider is that developed by Richard Christie (1976). Christie's work included the first means to include demographics to ascertain characteristics for potential jurors (Christie, 1976).

Concerning research regarding the scientific foundations for jury selection, there are pieces of literature that are available and currently endorsed by the American Psychological Association. This description fits that of the literature review conducted by Joel Lieberman and Bruce Sales (2006). The work is aimed at a compilation of historical and present literature as a means to assist forensic psychology consultants and legal professionals concerning jury selection (Lieberman & Sales, 2006). Likewise, another resource available is training programs for students that wish to follow a forensic psychology career path. For instance, depending on state laws, students who are currently perusing a Doctorate in Philosophy (Ph.D.) in Psychology or a Doctorate in Psychology (Psy. D) could earn a forensic psychology specialization. This, as well as similar programs, provide an opportunity to gain a specific focus in forensic psychology which can include risk and cognitive assessment, tests and measurements, and the practice of psychology in the court system. Lastly, students and forensic practitioners alike can gain knowledge of other resources in the form of conferences. These sessions are comprised of seminars such as the foundations and intricacies of the role of consulting and assisting in the jury selection process (American Psychology-Law Society, 2016). Overall, each resource provides a complementary approach to gain insights for jury selection consultation.

Consultation Preparation

Expertise Process

Before a forensic practitioner can become an expert, there are multiple steps to consider. The process to become an expert in each of these areas could initially require an interest recognition stemming from the practitioner. Later, it might be significantly relevant to identify the present need of these areas of expertise. This identification could include both regional necessity and current subfields that are seeking the expertise of a practitioner. Next, aspiring experts should become familiar with the many different requirements that might credit the individuals with meeting the standards of expertise. These provisions could include specific curriculum expectations, internship, specialized training, licensing, post-doctoral preparation, and ethical standards compliance. Indeed, psychologists might commonly practice consultation in specific fields ranging from cases involving business law (Hutson, 2007) to capital offenses. Communicating psychological concepts and their impacts to laypersons (Pittel et al., n.d.) and law enforcement (Kassin et al., 2010) should be a matter of consultation expertise as they relate to a given case. As such, these matters should be included in the expertise development process.

Issues with Consultation

The impacts of forensic psychology towards the legal system could be observed in one of the multiple roles practitioners can execute: consultation. As noted previously, this role consists of tasks such as providing expert testimony (Gottlieb & Coleman, 2012), conducting evaluations, and assisting lawyers in the jury selection process (Melton, Petrila, Poythress, & Slobogin, 2007). However, each of these skilled duties can pose ethical, legal, and practical issues and considerations for professionals. For instance, the necessary skill level, training, and expertise required for conducting expert witness role demands high standards, and correspondingly, similar remuneration (McKee, n.d.). As a result, this type of compensation could be presented as a concern by legal parties (Babitsky & Mangraviti, 2000), later to be conceptualized as an ethical violation or issue.

Another issue could be present when conducting evaluations of an examinee. However, the field of forensic psychology, given its relatively new development, might not count with extensive literature to support some evaluations (Shuman, Cunningham, Connell, & Reid, 2003), thus becoming a potential legal violation. Lastly, it has been argued that while working for an attorney during the jury selection stage, practitioners could be exposed to a practice issue. In this regard, attorneys might deem that practitioners who aided the jury selection process might also serve in another consultant task in the same case (Melton et al., 2007).

Importance of Concerns

Given the challenges these issues and concerns might provide to forensic psychology practitioners, it is relevant to discuss their importance. For example, it could be argued that if the compensation concern is not adequately addressed, then upcoming testimony and its preceding credibility might be put in jeopardy. As such, regardless of which level of expertise was used to achieve expert opinions, its value could be reduced for those who were granted access to its development. Conversely, lack of empirical support to conduct evaluations could be equally as inadequate. It has been noted that the mechanisms leading to testimony, such as how data is collected, should be substantiated by vindicated scientific foundations (Gottlieb & Coleman, 2012). Lastly, executing roles multiple consulting roles after duty selection might also put subsequent work at risk since it could be a significant source of bias (Melton et al., 2007).

Needs for the Subspecialties

After the relevance and use of psychological science in the field, professional organizations began the recognition of forensic psychology under its own merit (Edkins et al., 2017). However, the application of this field has extended beyond the mere use of behavioral science knowledge in a legal arena and general consultation. Rather, despite its recent development, forensic psychology has become an integral part of the legal process through implementation in multiple legal settings. As such, this text is set in providing a brief overview of the main subspecialties in which forensic psychology has been divided and the roles of forensic psychologists. In some instances, I will compare Federal laws with the Nation's first state in alphabetical order, Alabama, among others, as means to provide a comparison of the two levels of statutes. Readers are encouraged to consider how their local and national laws also impact the practice of forensic psychologists. I will present the interesting challenges and key topics that complete the field of forensic psychology.

Chapter 2: Civil Forensic Psychology

Overview

Major Roles and Responsibilities

The multiple areas of expertise in psychology and human behavior might be successfully applied in a scope of legal manners. The application of such field is noted in both civil and criminal courts, which will be covered in greater detail in another section. In regards to civil forensic psychology, practitioners might be called upon to perform a wide variety of roles. These tasks can include assisting legal professionals during a civil case along with providing expert witness testimony. For example, practitioners could provide significant information concerning child custody and child abuse evaluations (Bartol & Bartol, 2012). This type of work can stem from either parents' legal representatives or judicial professionals. As a result, forensic psychologists might make use of assessment tools and specialized training in order to serve a broad range of clients. Similarly, forensic psychologists could engage in the role of a researcher along the judicial process. In this sense, psychologists could utilize research and interview techniques for the selection of individuals that might adequately perform the duty of jurors (Bartol & Bartol, 2012).

Another pertinent role under the field of civil forensic psychology is that of an expert witness and competency to stand trial evaluations. Indeed, this responsibility in the civil court has been demonstrated and initially recognized during the second half of the 20th century (González-Sala et al., 2017). This role could make the psychologist responsible for conducting several evaluations. These steps might include that of assessing if prior psychological history might have played a role in executing the offense and how the illness might have an impact during the defendant's judicial process (Gianvanni & Sharman, 2017). Likewise, some practitioners might be requested to determine the likelihood of committing such offenses again (Andrés-Pueyo & Echeburúa, 2010).

Civil Case

Provided the range of expertise that psychologists are able to obtain, multiple practice areas might benefit from the field's contributions. Therefore, psychologists could perform forensic duties in manners of sexual harassment litigation. First, certain legal definitions relate to this civil case area that impact practitioner's duties. This form of aggravation can stem from verbal and non-verbal unwanted sexual behaviors (Bartol & Bartol, 2012). Along these lines, sexual harassment types have been defined under the United States Supreme Court system. For instance, when such unwelcomed sexual actions occur, it must be shown that it was executed as means obtain advancement or something in return (*Meritor Savings Bank v. Vinson*, 1986), also referred to as *quid pro quo* or "this for that."Another possible justification for sexual harassment cases is that it must be shown that the aggravation resulted in a hostile work environment (*Meritor Savings Bank v. Vinson*, 1986). Sexual harassment is a violation of civil rights since it is deemed a form of gender-based discrimination (Civil Rights Act of 1964). As a result, a person who has been exposed to this type of harassment is protected under this United States Labor Law. However, as it pertains more closely to forensic practitioners, in order to be deemed as psychologically significant in a court setting, such harassment should have resulted in a disorder beyond ordinary discomfort (Bartol & Bartol, 2012).

Forensic Psychology Professional Duties

As means to ascertain the distress from the event and their psychological outcomes, psychologists might be summoned to conduct evaluations. It must be noted that both the plaintiff and the defendant can request this service (Bartol & Bartol, 2012). A professional role of a forensic psychologist in this civil case area could include identifying prior sexual trauma history (Bartol & Bartol, 2012) and present psychological trauma due to the alleged harassment (Franklin, 2011b). The present trauma can result in psychological disorders such as depression (Franklin, 2011d) and it is still considered a form of harassment in the workplace even when no monetary or economic loss was present (*Meritor Savings Bank v. Vinson*, 1986). Consequently, forensic practitioners might execute the role of evaluators in this case. Another role psychologists might perform in this area is that of providing commentary on how reasonable the plaintiff's claim of harassment was (Franklin, 2011e). It is noteworthy to mention that in any case and in any court, *the court system, not the practitioner*, is to make that final determination (Franklin, 2011d).

Civil Case Reports

Arguably, one of the most significant responsibilities of a forensic practitioner is that of crafting a psychological report. This type of professional task serves pertinent functions based on its set referral questions. For instance, a primary essential function of forensic psychology reports and documentation is that of addressing specific referral questions. Although this function might appear somewhat trivial given the common understanding of the purpose of reports in general, this function must be considered on its own merit. Within the forensic scope, practitioners might potentially have to include aspects that directly relate to legal matters given their opinions (Melton, Petrila, Poythress, & Slobogin, 2007). A second function of the forensic report is that of enhancing the parties' knowledge of the client (Harvey, 2006; Melton et al., 2007). With this purpose in mind, legal professionals might use said knowledge to reach an agreement between the prosecution and the examinee concerning criminal cases, and other forms of resolution in the case of civil trials (Melton et al., 2007). Lastly, another function of these reports is that of potential prognoses and treatment recommendations. In this regard, practitioners could be tasked with ascertaining such recommendations. These, in turn, might later substantiate the examinee's future improvement (Harvey, 2006).

Reports and Documentation Importance

The importance forensic psychology reports and documentation in court settings could be explained through the obstacles that expert witnesses might experience during cross-examination. For instance, faulty documentation and substandard reports could lead to a platform (Melton et al., 2007) of evidence against the witness' knowledge and possible credibility. Additionally, the importance of both aspects of forensic writing is that they might limit how information is taken out of context (Babitsky & Mangraviti, 2000). Adequate documentation limits how one's testimony could be dismissed. Lack of such safeguard could result in the expert witness' impeachment (Babitsky & Mangraviti, 2000). Lastly, keeping records of the data, analysis, and conclusions could be considered adequate support for the hypotheses developed and presented during the case (Ackerman, 2006).

Similarities and Differences of the Evaluations

The extent of evaluations covered in a legal setting is perhaps equally correspondent to issues affecting each client and the law. As such, forensic psychology professionals could conduct a myriad of evaluations on civil and family courts. For instance, such evaluation is that of an individual's competency to handle their financial affairs. In this regard, these evaluations are focused in the determination of whether the examinee has the competency to independently engage in financial manners that could include a living will, and a last will and testament (Franklin, 2011a). Another similar evaluation is that of issues assessed by independent medical examinations (IMEs). Like those involving financial decision evaluations, IMEs also focus on the examinee's capacity to be competent (American Psychological Association, 2012). However, even though both evaluations could concern impairment provided by a disability, IMEs extend beyond financial issues and includes a significant impairment in the examinee's way of life (American Psychological Association, 2012). Contrary to these evaluations, evaluations concerning child custody issues not only involve one's competency to handle individual matters, but also the caretaking of a child (American Psychological Association, 2016ba). It could be argued that all three evaluations address competency as defined by a specific set of civil law.

Evaluation and Insights

Since each evaluation serves a defined concern, its use under specific circumstances sets their adequacy. For instance, an evaluation to address the competency to handle one's financial affairs could be necessary during expert testimony regarding a person's ability to manage investments and trusts (Franklin, 2011a). Arguably, IMEs could also extend to other forms of competency such as persons with a significant mental health disability. Here, certain persons within this population could be experiencing a reduced capacity for individual competency (Melton et al., 2007). As a result, practitioners could be needed to address a person's cognitive abilities such as reasoning and memory (Franklin, 2011a). Lastly, child custody evaluations could be included in cases where a mutual agreement between parents was not achieved (American Psychological Association, 2016ba). It must be noted that this type of need is only necessary in one out of ten cases (Melton et al., 2007).

Custody

Custody Cases

As noted, forensic psychologists might be called upon to provide their expertise to assist in other assessments involving civil court. As such, a psychologist might be faced with the task of child custody evaluations. This type of service not only involves complex techniques but various ethical concerns. In this section, I will present a scenario as means to evaluate potential child custody areas that might include further ethical considerations. The case study shows a possible issue of infidelities by the husband's doing as alleged by the mother but adamantly rejected by the father. Furthermore, the mother also states that the children are aware of such affairs and have also met one of the individuals with whom the husband supposedly had an extramarital affair. The second area to address is that of the relationship between and care of the parents towards the children. Based on the second issue, the mother requested that the father leave the family home, which has resulted in a separation between him and the children. Here, the husband contends that he has not been able to partake in duties that he alleges he engaged with the children, such as taking the minors to extracurricular activities and to receive medical care. Lastly, a potential area to call attention to is that of the parent's cultural background. As presented in the case study, the ethnic and racial makeup of the parents is that of African American and Caucasian multiracial familial relationship, for the father and mother respectively. Provided these custody areas, I will make use of ethical guidelines as a means to explain and address why each might be considered a custody issue.

Guideline Application

Each of these areas warrants further evaluation given the ethical concerns that might be present for forensic psychologists. The first area could be addressed via the 10th guideline for practitioners. This guideline proposes that psychologists should make use of multiple sources of information and data gathering before informing custody opinions (American Psychological Association, 2016ba). In such regard, it has been noted that more than seldomly, the minors are not particularly engaged during the child custody evolutions (Bartol & Bartol, 2012). Consequently, the children might become a valuable source of information regarding this issue. The second issue of children caretaking is exemplified under guideline number six. The services psychologists provided under such evaluations should be founded on both substantial literature and possible collaboration of colleagues (American Psychological Association, 2016ba). In this case, a practitioner should make use of evidence and collected to ascertain who might be more suited to address the paternal needs and caretaking of the children (American Psychological Association, 2016ba), via guidance and psychological proximity (Franklin, 2011c). The last issue could be contemplated with the recommendations of the first guideline. In this sense, psychologists are advised to examine cultural considerations that might be pertinent to this process (American Psychological Association, 2016ba). These practices might assist in bias reduction (Bartol & Bartol, 2012) and adequate evaluations.

Custody Assessment

The impacts of forensic assessment extend beyond those in a criminal and correctional setting. In the civil psychology arena, forensic professionals could be tasked with child custody evaluations. This process could be a considerably difficult task since the legal system, minors, and extensive assessments are an inherent part of custody processes. These matters could include assessments, interviews, and potential recommendations that come from such evaluations. Therefore, it is imperative that practitioners consider some of the issues that could arise in especially difficult custody processes, which is especially the case in high-profile cases. Here, there are certain areas a forensic psychology professional should take into consideration when providing a recommendation. For instance, if the evaluations involve high-profile persons, media involvement could be expected. In this case, practitioners could be exposed to outside information that does not stem from standardized evaluations, thus jeopardizing assessment interpretations. However, practitioners are recommended to make use of protocols and assessment tools that pertain to the custody case at hand (Zumbach & Koglin, 2015). Additionally, high-profile cases might involve assessment of the current caregivers (Patel & Choate, 2014). In such cases, the examinees might present underreporting of clinical personality issues (Resendes & Lecci, 2012), or "fake good." An instrument to address such concerns is the Minnesota Multiphasic Personality Inventory-2 (MMPI-2). This instrument allows the practitioner to gather data of underreporting and validity scales, such as the "Lie" scale (Butcher et al., 2001) that could provide information on potential clinical issues (Resendes & Lecci, 2012).

Chapter 3: Criminal Forensic Psychology

Overview

Major Roles and Responsibilities

Amongst the variety of subspecialties within the forensic psychology field is that of criminal forensic psychology. This subspecialty refers to addressing criminal conduct via means of providing interventions or treatment; and perhaps prevention to mitigate such behavior (Bartol & Bartol, 2012). In this regard, the overlap between general psychology and forensic psychology can be observed since intervention strategies are commonly associated with the former field. As such, it could be argued that the roles within criminal psychology are similar to those in a general field. In the criminal psychology area, practitioners execute specialty roles such as conducting research with both juveniles and adults (Bartol & Bartol, 2012). There are two potential primary outcomes of the role of researcher for practitioners. First, one responsibility is making use of research as means to prevent criminal behavior (Bartol & Bartol, 2012). Secondly, a forensic specialist might also mitigate this conduct via policy development and address a person with potential mental health illnesses (Bartol & Bartol, 2012). In this case, a forensic psychologist might serve as an advisor in multiple settings such as in government, criminal, and school environments (Bartol & Bartol, 2012).

Case Law Description

The inherent correspondence between the law and forensic psychology has stemmed from many historical case laws and other rulings. A possible significant example to consider is that of *Milton Dusky v. United States.* Here, the Supreme Court was presented with a case review. The contention held that, as defendants, having an awareness of the charges was not sufficient for adequate competency (Bartol & Bartol, 2012). As a result, the United States held that persons should be able to assist in their defense via current ability to comprehend the legal process and consultation (*Dusky v. U.S.*, 1960). This ruling ultimately resulted in Dusky's new hearing, where the individual's competency at that time was to be re-evaluated once again, as mandated by the Supreme Court (*Dusky v. U.S.*, 1960). This then newly-ordered matter provided an expanded view of the concept of competency as understood in the court of law and the field of forensic psychology.

Forensic Psychology Influence

This case law's impact ultimately affected forensic psychology in practice. The established Dusky standard, referring to both having the awareness and ability to aid in one's defense (Bartol & Bartol, 2012), demanded an expansion of forensic psychological duties. For example, psychologists had to consider a person's potential impairments in regards to the competency standard (Pirelli, Zapf, & Gottdiener, 2011). Furthermore, these considerations provided a foundation for empirically-based research for competency assessment. As a result, practitioners developed instruments that took into account the Dusky standard along with psychological matters that could play a role during the legal process (Pirelli et al., 2011).

Insanity and Forensic Psychology

Importance of Legal Definitions

One mechanism used by societies to maintain its working and civil status is the application of justice to impart warranted and fitting punishments. However, the determination of finding an individual guilty might not necessarily imply mere culpability. The recognition that some individuals might have specific circumstances, such as their mental state during an offense, extends far beyond recent years. Indeed, since the second half of the 19th century, persons who acted upon the impacts of being "mad" might have deemed them as not responsible for the crimes that have committed while in that state (Winslow, 1854). It argued that their actions did not align necessarily with logical conclusions since their symptoms affected the individual's reasoning transgressions (Winslow, 1854). Presently, two significant standards examine such evaluation when people are considered guilty or not guilty. This is the case of the insanity evaluations as presented by the American Law Institute (ALI) and M'Naghten standard as used by, among others, the state of Alabama in thE United States. For instance, both of the standards propose that there are indeed individuals are not culpable of their actions due to mental health conditions and symptomatic expression that is directly impacting a crime (Melton, Petrila, Poythress, & Slobogin, 2007). Furthermore, another similarity is that both standards consider that individuals might have a limited understanding of wrongfulness of the crime (Alabama Criminal Code § 13A-3-1, 2016; Melton et al., 2007). Yet, an important difference among both definitions is that the ALI's classification might also include persons that cannot remain within the confines of the law as consistent with insanity (Melton et al., 2007). Conversely, this is not the case in the state of Alabama, where the individual must demonstrate both the impacts of the mental health illness and their inability to comprehend the wrongdoing (Alabama Criminal Code § 13A-3-1, 2016), not the defendant's potential inability to be law-abiding (Yakush & Wolbransky, 2013).

Impacts towards Forensic Practitioners

The relevance and importance of legal definitions to the forensic psychology professional could be examined through their roles. For example, such practitioners could be assigned to assist in the selection of jurors where a possible insanity defense might be taking place. Researchers Louden and Skeem (2007) found that jurors presented with this type of defense might ultimately follow their pre-determined prototypes of insanity rather than utilizing the definitions and instructions presented by the court. Consequently, the definitions of insanity might affect how the practitioner selects members of the jury as a means to reduce juror bias. Thousands of proceedings in the United States have declared defendants as "not guilty by reason of insanity" ([NGRI]; Gowensmith, Murrie, Boccaccini, & McNichols, 2017) which might have been impacted by this form of bias. Additionally, practitioners assisting during an insanity defense evaluation might play an instrumental role during such determination. In a court setting, the jury might make use of the practitioner's assessment of the defendant in favor of such defense (Kalis & Meynen, 2014). It can be concluded that the definition used at any given case could ultimately affect, how peers are selected, how evaluations are conducted and the contributions of the practitioners when applying the law.

Legal Differences of Insanity

Undoubtedly, the legal definition utilized in a court of law could yield different outcomes of a particular case. In this section, I will introduce the case study of Jeffrey Dahmer, who was accused of nearly 20 murders; where multiple individuals had been cannibalized and sexually exploited. Inside of Dahmer's residence, investigators recovered body parts and mangled corpses; many of which were mutilated while the individuals were still alive. The evidence noted that Dahmer had made mutilations as means to use the body parts and corpses for sexual acts. Upon psychological evaluation, a practitioner suggested that the defendant was unable to stop these acts given a strong sexual desire towards these types of crimes. It could be argued that an insanity plea might indeed be warranted on this case study. However, these definitions could vary based on a federal level or with other meanings for insanity. As a result, I will examine the two legal definitions of insanity as a means to analyze their possible impacts in this case study.

First, the legal definition of insanity, in a federal context, notes that individuals who attempt such defense should have had a psychological illness that directly impaired their ability to discern the consequences of their acts (U.S.C. § 4241). Furthermore, just the history or diagnosis of psychological disorders does not substantiate an insanity defense (U.S.C. § 4241). In this case study, it could be reasonably inferred that Dahmer was aware of the consequences of his acts since the defendant hid the evidence that could have supported his prosecution. Furthermore, the practitioners did not appear to have reached a consensus on the relationship between his psychological illnesses and Dahmer's criminal actions. As a result, based on this particular definition, the defendant's insanity plea might not have been applicable. In contrast, the insanity definition of the Model Penal Code (MPC) by the American Law Institute (ALI) might have resulted in a different outcome. The ALI's insanity definition notes that the individuals have a psychological illness that either affects their ability to comprehend the extent of their crimes or whose behavior cannot adhere to the law. In this regard, Dahmer's sexual compulsion towards illegal acts, given his psychological illness, might have rendered him insane due to his inability to conform to legal boundaries.

Similarly, another case to consider is that of Andrea Yates in the early 2000's. This case included the murder of her five young children, which Yates claimed she had committed due to a supernatural satanic command (West & Lichtenstein, 2006). Initially, Yates was found guilty despite a history of hallucinations, and a majority consensus of insane state (McLellan, 2006). This case proved to be significant since one of the practitioners, working for the prosecution, noted that Yates was not criminally insane (McLellan, 2006). The practitioner's expert testimony was contended as he provided consultation for a television show where a woman was found criminally insane under the same charges (McLellan, 2006). For this reason, Yates' defense argued that the expert witness provided false testimony since their client was indeed found insane by the practitioner (Yates, 2005). As a result, the verdict was considered a mistrial and was reversed (Yates, 2005).

Legal Conclusions

The legal definitions in both case studies played a significant role in influencing the cases' outcomes. When considering the federal definition of insanity, Dahmer could have been judged and held accountable for his crimes. This legal outcome stands opposed to the ALI's insanity definition, given Dahmer's powerlessness to confound to legal guidelines. In Yates case, the legal definition of insanity contributed to the verdict in multiple aspects. For instance, the defense initially argued an insanity plea. However, this reasonable insanity defense was trumped given the expert witness's apparent lack of ethical behavior. Secondly, it could be suggested that the judge allowed another proceeding (Yates, 2005) since the insanity evaluation by the other practitioners was justified and should have been considered once again.

Standing Trial

Hypothetical Examples

To follow along with the implications of forensic evaluations, I will be presenting two scenarios with individuals who could potentially be considered incompetent to stand trial. The first scenario includes Mr. G, a recently separated combat veteran who was medically discharged due to Posttraumatic Stress Disorder and Brief Psychotic Disorder. Mr. G confronted Ms. Z, his neighbor, due to vehicles blocking his garage entrance. Ms. Z responded that her party guests would move the vehicles; a conversation that escalated into an altercation. Witnesses noted that Ms. Z threw a chair at Mr. G when he apparently attempted to assault her physically. Two male party guests, including Mr. Pérez, separated them from the fight. Mr. G went to his house and then returned to the party guests and his neighbor. Mr. G allegedly attempted to shoot Ms. Z, but Mr. Pérez interceded and sustained fatal injuries from the discharge. The second scenario includes Mrs. Smith, who has worked as an attorney for nearly 35 years. Recently, Mrs. Smith has been accused by one of her clients of inadequate notary services that resulted in the client's loss of property.

Mrs. Smith's attorneys state that she then and now lacks the current mental state to be aware of her alleged crime due to early onset dementia.

Incompetency Rationale

The competency scenarios of Mr. G. and Mrs. Smith could be further evaluated under the federal definition of competency. This definition notes a two-fold consideration. First, as with the case of Mr. G., this individual was judged to be incompetent as a result of mental diseases that limit his understanding of the nature and consequences of the proceedings (U.S.C. § 4241). Furthermore, Mr. G's competency to stand trial could be based upon the charges presented against him which could be part of a lengthy trial (Bartol & Bartol, 2012). In the second scenario, it could be argued that Mrs. Smith is not able to properly assist in her defense (U.S.C. § 4241). In this regard, Mrs. Smith might be considered currently incompetent for this preceding as after being formally evaluated (*Dusky v. U.S.*, 1960).

Ethical Dilemmas and Challenges

A forensic psychology professional might be exposed to significant challenges while working in the criminal scope. There are multiple ethical considerations such as potential biases that the practitioner might have when considering criminal behavior. For example, scholars argue that practitioners might confound cultural background with socioeconomic factors that might impact criminal behavior (Goodman, 2012). As a result, it could be argued that all aspects of the criminal psychology role of research, prevention, evaluation, and treatment could be jeopardized. Further, this bias might result in a potentially controversial manner, as the wrongful association of the two factors might lead to a disservice towards disadvantaged groups. This dilemma could be addressed through familiarization of the literature concerning the specific demographic the practitioners intend to serve.

Another ethical issue that practitioners might face is the interaction of developing or providing treatment while considering the legal requirements of such interventions. For instance, a practitioner might work in a setting where a legal matter sets limits or requirements for treatment that a practitioner might be opposed to (Day & Casey, 2009). As a result, a psychologist is presented with the ethical dilemma between what is required in a criminal forensic psychology setting versus that stemming from the presenting issues. This difficulty could be addressed by consulting what alternate, but equivalent, treatment might be provided to the client while abiding by legal and ethical standards.

Chapter 4: Juvenile Forensic Psychology

Overview

Major Roles and Responsibilities

Another significant layer to add to the diverse duties that forensic practitioners might face is that of the age of the client. Undoubtedly, the age of those involved in a forensic setting might have a significant impact when offense charges have occurred. In a juvenile setting, a psychologist might be summoned to provide assessment, assistance (Gianvanni & Sharman, 2017), and clinical evaluations in a court of law (Guarnera, Murrie, & Boccaccini, 2017). For example, a forensic psychologist could be asked to conduct an assessment as to whether the juvenile comprehends the extent and repercussions of the alleged offense and the social norms that govern such act. Another role involves assisting within the court setting by determining if there are mitigating variables (Gianvanni & Sharman, 2017) that could become a factor between a juvenile and regular court trial. Lastly, a role psychologists might engage in is that of conducting clinical evaluations. This type of evaluation can include suicide risk; particularly with young, first-time offenders.

Contemporary Juvenile Forensic Issues

Forensic psychologists might be exposed to multiple challenges based on the populations they serve. These issues might become somewhat more complicated when considering the particular setting in which practitioners conduct their duties. Such is the case of assessment within juvenile forensic psychology. During its early historical development, it was held that young persons should be placed in a juvenile setting as a way to promote rehabilitation (Bartol & Bartol, 2012). However, contemporary areas of concern might pose an issue regarding young offenders' rehabilitation. For example, a possible concern to address is the assessment for recovery and potential re-offenses of juvenile sex offenders. It has been noted that the process is used for identifying the individual's possible threat to the greater community (Bartol & Bartol, 2012). Arguably, using assessment for such purposes is undoubtedly a difficult task. Yet, this type of evaluation might become limited based on poor research assumptions (Zimring et al., 2009) and limited empirical data to address such populations (The John D. and Catherine T. MacArthur Foundation, 2006).

Importance and Addressing Areas of Concern

The importance of addressing assessment with juvenile sex offenders is based on the limited literature available to serve such purpose, the highly complex nature of the assessment, and the impacts the findings might have towards the young offender and society. First, the literature gap regarding rehabilitation and future offenses poses a potential disservice to the juvenile sex offender and the Juvenile Forensic discipline. It has been noted that both practitioners and laypersons might have negative unsubstantiated assumptions of societal threats and recidivism (Zimring et al., 2009). As a result, the young offender might receive substandard evaluations due to insufficient empirical data; as well as poor practitioner judgment and interpretation of findings. Secondly, although it was acknowledged that juvenile offenders should be provided with services that cater to a young client's needs, this task proved to be more difficult than initially expected (The John D. and Catherine T. MacArthur Foundation, 2006). Consequently, practitioners are highly advised to gather a broad range of sources of information, such as previous violence and school data as means to conduct proper juvenile sex offender assessment (Bartol & Bartol, 2012).

Lastly, forensic psychologists should exert caution when providing recommendations (Bartol & Bartol, 2012) since it has been noted that a history of juvenile sex offending does not inherently translate into re-occurrence or offenses as an adult (Zimring et al., 2009). Along the lines of cautious data gathering and appropriate recommendations, forensic practitioners can make use of other techniques and resources to mitigate poor assessment with a juvenile sex offending population. For instance, a psychologist could incorporate other venues that could offer potential rehabilitation. These include juvenile-oriented agencies that provide eclectic services for those who are deemed suitable for treatment (The John D. and Catherine T. MacArthur Foundation, 2006).

Controversial Issues

Relevant Research

Forensic professionals in the subspecialty juvenile forensic psychology could be faced with a myriad of challenges that can include training considerations, specific assessment, and report development. For example, providing services to a juvenile population could inherently require particular training as means to adequately address this population. However, despite the fact that receiving such training could be relatively common, scholars suggest that such formation remains to be recurrently substandard (Guarnera et al., 2017). Additionally, principally with a juvenile population, practitioners should be mindful when considering specified assessment and juveniles. This recommendation is based on literature findings where juveniles who have a prior history of committing sexual offenses are not *de facto* likely to re-offend (Zimring et al., 2009). Furthermore, judicial professionals also note significant issues once they receive assessment reports. Here, these experts point out dissatisfaction with such reports given the psychologist's use of templates or when they make use of sections used for other client's reports (Gianvanni & Sharman, 2017). Further, it has been noted that the variability between juveniles that have committed sexual offenses might constitute a highly diversified group (van Wijk et al., 2005). Certainly, these challenges could be mitigated by proper education and training formation regarding juvenile assessment.

Case Study and State's Juvenile Justice

Across the subspecialties of psychology, perhaps one of the more relevant factors to consider is the client's age. More importantly, age-specific laws could also be of much relevance when considering forensic issues. As means to evaluate this case study, I will make use of the laws, rules, and regulations as devised by the State of Alabama. As such, the age of the alleged perpetrator and the victim is the first regulation to consider and will be evaluated under *Juvenile Proceedings*. Here, the case at hand is based on a young male who was accused of shooting and killing a female. The 14-year-old male was identified by the victim's spouse and later confessed to the crime upon police apprehension. Similarly, the age of the suspect plays a significant factor in possibly transferring the case to a juvenile court (Alabama Code §12-15-203, 2016). Additionally, some states also take into consideration the psychological health of the minor. For instance, a forensic evaluation could be conducted as means to determine if they should be tried as an adult (Alabama Code §12-15-203, 2016). The second regulation to consider is those relevant to case rulings in the state where the juvenile will face prosecution. For instance, some states pose that the age of the victim (*Taylor v. State*, 2004) could be viewed as an aggravating factor for the crime. Yet, a significant variable to address is the suspect's age as it relates to his confession (*Burks v. State*, 1991).

Codes-Case Study Relationship

It could be argued that the adolescent's confession might not have occurred while his rights were being upheld. Based on the state of the scenario's law, *Burks v. State* (1991), a person younger than 18 years of age at the time of the arrest should be informed about rights that pertain to him as a minor; such as consulting his parents before confession. For this discussion and based on the case study, the confession will be considered as valid as a forensic psychologist was consulted. In this scenario, if the individual is found to have a psychological impairment, then the adolescent could be trialed in a juvenile court (Alabama Code §12-15-203, 2016). If, however, such is not the case, then the nature of the crime and the age of the victim play a significant role in this case study. For instance, if the individual is accused to have committed first-degree murder in Alabama, he is considered to be an adult if the offense occurred at the age of 14 (Alabama Code §12-15-203, 2016). Furthermore, the defense might be limited in attempting to address mitigating factors that could justify a juvenile case. This state has ruled that murders committed against elderly individuals, 60 years old or older, could be considered as aggravated (*Taylor v. State*, 2004). In this case study, a 14-year-old's sentence as an adult for the first-degree offense could be life in prison (Alabama Criminal Code §13A-5-43.2, 2016).

Sentences

Prison vs. Community Supervision

It can be argued that crimes committed by minors might compel some into considering faults in multiple social institutions. However, socially-based institutions might be able to serve as means to address crimes and reform delinquent juveniles. In fact, this idea was the foundation of developing correctional facilities for juveniles. The original intent was to create a setting, separate from those of adults, to assist in the juvenile's reform while catering to age-specific needs (The John D. and Catherine T. MacArthur Foundation, 2006). Presently, this objective might not be considered in the same fashion. Mainly, some persons might propose that more severe crimes, such as first-degree murder, might warrant that a juvenile be tried and sentenced as an adult. This proposal might not be entirely supported by research that compares that type of sentencing with alternate methods such as community supervision. For instance, literature suggests that younger convicts that have been placed in a prison setting might be exposed to greater violence threats (Kolivoski & Shook, 2016). In turn, this specific population then could engage in actions that could result in both behavioral and psychological issues such as in-prison transgressions and stress (Kolivoski & Shook, 2016).

On the other hand, community supervision might reduce such risk *de facto* as the juvenile inherently would not be placed in such setting. Further, it could be argued that a juvenile placed on community supervision might not be exposed to coercion and violent behavior from other inmates such as committing other crimes in the facility. Additionally, juveniles in community supervision can engage in rehabilitation in manners that might not be available or might be comparatively different to those in prison (Greene & Evelo, 2013). These opportunities include an academic environment, employment, and integration with the general community.

Juvenile vs. Criminal Court

After considering the differences between a prison setting versus community supervision setting, it is relevant to consider the risk factors for juvenile offenders being tried and sentenced as adults. The pertinence of evaluating this population and the risks they might face can foundationally stem from the increase of harsher sentences towards juveniles. Recently, there has been an increase in juveniles that have been given life in prison sentences (Carmichael & Burgos, 2012) and similar non-juvenile punishments. This type of sentencing has been suggested to bring some risk for juvenile offenders. For example, some risks include those of possible psychological harm. These issues could include a higher risk for depression, the potentiality of self-harm and attempting suicide (Kolivoski & Shook, 2016). Further, even when sentences are completed, the potential risks extend beyond those within the adult correctional facility. For instance, juveniles who were tried as adults could be at greater risk of re-offending (Kolivoski & Shook, 2016). Additionally, when such criminal offenses occur, the risk of committing different and more severe crimes becomes more plausible (Kolivoski & Shook, 2016).

Forensic Psychology Professional's Roles

There is a myriad of roles and responsibilities that could be found throughout the juvenile process. Forensic psychology professionals could be able to satisfy such needs via the roles of examiner, evaluator, and therapist. For instance, a psychologist might conduct examinations to assist in the determination of transferring a younger defendant between a juvenile or an adult court system (Means, Heller, & Janofsky, 2012). This role could be based, in part, on the defendant's potential for treatment in either correctional facility (Kolivoski & Shook, 2016). Secondly, psychologists could conduct evaluations that could help in assessing whether the juvenile offender might be a good candidate for rehabilitation programs that cater to developmental needs (Calamari Productions, 2012). In this sense, practitioners with the proper training and experience could provide therapeutic rehabilitation to a qualifying juvenile. It can be argued that some of this need might be founded in how laypersons have become confident about the positive results of this type of rehabilitation (Greene & Evelo, 2013). Interestingly, part of this process might entail examination and evaluations outside of the judicial system. Therefore, forensic psychologists could conduct mental health evaluations for treatment progression for those who have been deemed to benefit from community service (Reich, 2014).

Chapter 5: Law Enforcement, Investigative, and Correctional Psychology

Police Psychology

Major Roles and Responsibilities

Forensic practitioners have also provided applicable contributions to law enforcement authorities. In the subspecialty field of police psychology, psychologists provide a broad range of services based on administrative, analytical, and therapy roles. For example, psychologists might be asked to conduct administrative work regarding potential force recruitment. In this sense, practitioners could provide personality and other forms as assessment as means to identify desired skills sets and traits necessary for law enforcement such as remaining calm. Besides the human resources aspect of working in police psychology, practitioners could be asked to execute other analytical roles. On this subject, professionals could be responsible for developing profiles of offenders (Bartol & Bartol, 2012). Another significant role that practitioners might engage in is the development of support systems, training to address mental health illness and counseling services (Bartol & Bartol, 2012) within a therapeutic role.

Forensic professionals engage in multiple functions within a police setting. These roles are just as varied as the populations they intend to serve. As such, it is relevant to consider how the roles and responsibilities of forensic psychology professionals are impacted given discrimination laws. Such is the case of the Americans with Disabilities Act of 1990. In a general sense, this law notes that individuals are not to be discriminated against on the basis of physical and psychological, and other forms of disabilities (Bartol & Bartol, 2012). The relevance of this law spans across many of the forensic psychologist's roles to include training and skills development of law enforcement personnel. For example, within the trainer role, practitioners should not generalize on the accommodations and needs required in servicing a group that includes an individual with a particular disability (American Psychological Association, 1996). Furthermore, a forensic psychologist in this role might also have to provide specialized training officers regarding their compliance with ADA standards. For instance, psychologists could provide tools and techniques to officers as means to address persons with disabilities related to mental health that might be in distress or that need to be taken into custody. The importance of providing such training is that it allows enhanced security protection for all the parties involved as well as reducing legal liabilities and ADA violations (Bartol & Bartol, 2012).

Employment in Law Enforcement

As previously noted, the incorporation of ADA in the police psychology-trainer relationship appears to be of significant importance in a trainer role; it might also be significant during the recruitment process. Indeed, a considerable portion of a practitioner's responsibilities revolves around the recruitment process for prospective law enforcement recruits. Therefore, forensic psychologists working in the police subspecialty in the screening and selection of candidates should consider the relevance of ADA and this process. For instance, during the pre-employment phase (Hibler, 2002), practitioners might be summoned to assist in the screening process for new personnel (Bartol & Bartol, 2012). However, it could be argued that psychologists should incorporate ADA standards when conducting such tasks. For instance, it could be noted that there is a legal component to such inclusion which addresses the essential roles entailed for such positions (U.S. EEOC, 2017) and whether a reasonable accommodation can be provided (Bartol & Bartol, 2012). Consequently, a practitioner should carefully examine the pertinent duties that might be expected to be fulfilled during a police officer's career. Furthermore, there could be an ethical component regarding the task of screening and ADA inclusion. For example, upon screening procedures development, a forensic psychologist might be encouraged to assess what resources are available for accommodation and how plausible such inclusion might be (American Psychological Association, 1996) in a police setting.

ERT Forensic Contributions

There are multiple agencies which have missions specifically focused on emergency response. One such agency, which I have had the opportunity to serve in for nearly ten years, is the intelligence field within the federal government. Many of the intelligence emergency response teams are usually focused on the on-the-scene reconnaissance, interview, interrogation, and intelligence exploitation of an ongoing offender, insurgent, or terrorist attack. Since much of the intelligence analysis depends on behavior and pattern examination, an overlap with the psychological field might be warranted. For such reason, it could be argued that there is a need for the contributions that forensic psychology professionals might offer towards Intelligence ERT. For instance, forensic psychology professionals working in police subspecialty might be able to provide useful training (Bartol & Bartol, 2012) and resources as means to conduct intelligence analysis. For example, crime psychologists receive information from a myriad of sources that later are condensed in order to perform appropriate data exploitation. Furthermore, this type of forensic contribution might later assist in focusing the investigation towards certain offenders, thus facilitating the investigative process. As a result, Intelligence ERTs are able to receive adequate training from a forensic psychological professional, apply learned skills, and incorporate forensic psychology professional staff during the emergency response.

Findings for ERT

Although practitioners might offer many contributions towards the Intelligence ERT, such help could be founded on previous research findings. There are multiple areas that support literature findings and hence assist forensic psychology professionals working with this response team. First, social and cognitive foundations have benefited the development of police psychology. Mainly, scholars note that the research conducted in these fields provided insights via adequate framing of interrogation and interview questions. Another research focus regarding emergency response is that of organizational psychology. The findings within this field could be applied in emergency response context; such as how first responders react to a particularly high-risk situation. Additionally, such research is later applied in operational support (Hibler, 2002), providing an encompassing role of Intelligence ERT, forensic psychology, and improved understanding of the offense (Bartol & Bartol, 2012).

Military Psychology

Forensic Psychologists and Military Settings

Arguably one of the most challenging tasks practitioners might face is that of working in the military subspecialty role in hostile settings. Such areas of practice might include warfare/theater and detainee camps while assisting in interrogation. Multiple legal issues and ethical concerns arise when this role is not executed per practice boundaries. For example, forensic psychology professionals are not to perform or facilitate interrogation that is considered "enhanced"; which has been previously conducted in the history of the United States (American Psychological Association, 2017a). It must be noted that there are federal laws and international agreements that currently prohibit inhumane practices to include this form of interrogation. For instance, forensic practitioners that currently work as an employee must not engage in abuse; which could be prosecuted based on abusive actions (U.S. Department of Justice, 2006). Furthermore, forensic psychologists employed as contractors or those who have agreed to work under armed forces jurisdiction in a time of war, are bounded to not engage in torturous or cruel treatment while serving (Uniform Code of Military Justice, 1950). In such case, forensic psychologists might be prosecuted under military law. Another issue with engaging in illegal practices of enhanced interrogation is its possible violation of the international humanitarian law. In accordance with the Geneva Conventions (1950), forensic practitioners providing welfare services or working as civilians in times of conflict might be bounded to its legal limits. As such, if professionals are executing cruel or damaging the dignity of those they are working with; it is punishable by international rulings (Geneva Conventions, 1950).

Military vs. Civilian Practice

Besides the military/civilian duality that forensic psychologists are exposed to in military psychology, there are other peculiar issues to consider. There are various important differences between practicing in a military context that juxtapose those in a civilian setting. First, military psychologists, as well as the rest of the service members, are bounded by oath to defend and abide by the mandates of the officers appointed over them and the current presidency. Therefore, the needs of the higher authorities will supersede those of the clients (Zur & González, 2002). However, it could be argued that civilian psychologists exposed to ethical dilemmas or concerns need not abide by a set standard that cannot be addressed by an ethics committee or in a court of law. Another significant difference is authority perception. In a civilian setting, it could be argued that the practitioner holds a position of authority towards their clients. In a military context, a client might outrank the practitioner, regardless if they in a direct supervisory position over the psychologist. Further, the high rank most military psychologists will earn given their education and role will inherently provide them with authority to provide evidence and support for demotions, promotions, military disciplinary actions, and loss of employment of their military clients (Zur & González, 2002). In a civilian context, particularly in a court setting, practitioners might rarely have a final authority when addressing a client's fitness and liberties.

Controversial Issues and Challenges

Some challenges encountered by the forensic psychology professionals in the police and military subspecialty include the adequate and ethical performance of law enforcers while on duty. A psychologist might have the responsibility of training police officers concerning at-risk populations as suspects. In the case of the former, much critique has risen between racial and ethnic minorities given racial profiling (Edkins et al., 2017). In the event of the latter, law enforcers have been faced with much opposition regarding the potential coercion they might engage in during the interrogation and confession stages of investigations (Edkins et al., 2017). Indeed, research has noted that officers, based on their training, might potentially lead others into bias, thus receiving information that the law enforcer had already perceived about the suspect (Sweet, Meissner, & Atkinson, 2017). However, forensic psychology professionals might be able to address this concern via research and community outreach programs as means to mitigate negative myths surrounding law enforcement (Shaw et al., 2013). Likewise, practitioners have attempted to address the problem of faulty interrogation by introducing forms to frame questions to gain better interviews.

Investigative Forensic Psychology

Major Roles and Responsibilities

Another significant forensic subspecialty to consider is investigative psychology. The roles and responsibilities include determining the overall and individual's scope of the suspect's psychological state and characteristics, as well as profiling. For example, a psychologist could attempt to understand the person's viewpoint of the crime as it relates to the actions that were surrounding the offense (Canter & Youngs, 2012). Consequently, psychologists in this subspecialty may have the task of identifying the suspects' characteristics that pertain to their persona as well as that during the crime. In this regard, practitioners might have the role of a profiler; where crime scene and psychological profiling make take place (Bartol & Bartol, 2012). During the profiling development, forensic practitioners could make use of inferred behaviors that come from the crime scene as means to craft a profile (Bartol & Bartol, 2012).

The Validity of Criminal Profiling

Amongst the multiple areas of work that forensic psychologists might execute, it can be contended that criminal profiling is perhaps one of the most commonly portrayed ones in the media. Despite this arguable glorification, there are important considerations for profiling such as the information used for such analysis, and the strengths and limitations that follow after its use. Criminal profiling could be considered an ongoing process that attempts to provide a possible description of the offender and an approximation of how subsequent offenses might occur (Bartol & Bartol, 2012). Some researchers note that its rigor was not established until that the 1990s in Europe when the scientific method was used to determine profiling validity. Perhaps the most significant aspect of profiling is the information gathered to create such intricate work. The importance of profiling validity rests upon the inherent positive relationship between erroneous information that results in inadequate profiling. Therefore, I will discuss the possible strengths and shortcomings of making use of this tool based information/research on which the criminal profile is based.

Profiling Limitations

Criminal profiling relies on multiple sources of information, such as previous offender research and crime scene analysis. For instance, practitioners could make use of previous literature regarding offenders that have committed similar offenses to those they are developing a profile for (Bartol & Bartol, 2012). However, many practitioners and peers alike note that a possible limitation regarding the use of previous research as a foundation for criminal profiling revolves around confirmation bias. Here, it is proposed that despite practitioners having pertinent information that might dispute or support statements within the profile; the profiler might ignore those that contradict previously conceived ideas of the offender (Bartol & Bartol, 2012). The other potential source of information for profiling includes crime scene analysis. In this regard, the information collected during the crime scene investigation is used as means to evaluate offender characteristics and determine the possible suspects that could potentially match such profile. Yet, certain individuals might commit crimes while purposely taking this familiar pattern in mind and change their behaviors; resulting in a more complicated crime analysis-profile derivation.

Strengths and Investigative Tools

On the other hand, profiling provides some benefits to the agencies it might serve. For instance, some strengths of profiling include the condensing of vast amounts of information as means to focus the investigation towards key individuals. Another potential strength of profiling rests on its potential to provide accurate offender information where crime appears to be difficult to address (Knox, Limbacher, & McMahan, 1993). However, the use of criminal profiling as a tool of investigative psychology might be considered with caution. For example, it might be more adequate to use profiling when profilers base their analyses on current literature to substantiate their propositions (Bartol & Bartol, 2012). Otherwise, the use of criminal profiling might be based on non-empirical foundations and unsubstantiated data.

Supporting Evidence

Empirically Based Evidence

The conjunctions of multiple pieces of evidence assist in the understanding of a case. However, such sources of information should stem from valid and reliable evidence. This rationale is based on setting a scientific parameter that differentiates unsubstantiated claims that probably lead to wrongful conclusions. This is where empirically based evidence (EBE) comes into the legal arena. For instance, the importance of obtaining information from EBE is built upon legal standards and prior forensic research. Here, as discussed earlier, the Supreme Court case ruling of *Daubert v. Merrell Dow Pharmaceuticals* (1993) notes that those sources of information presented in the court of law should originate from literature generally agreed upon the scientific community specializing in such field. As a result, the testimony should be substantiated by empirically based evidence that was upheld through scientific scrutiny. This idea brings the importance of EBE to prior forensic research. It has been noted that persons that work under the investigative psychology subspecialty might wrongfully provide information that was built upon confirmation bias (Bartol & Bartol, 2012). This disposition might lead experts to focus solely on sources of information that support their preconceived conclusions despite the existence of evidence that supports the contrary (Bartol & Bartol, 2012). As such, making use of EBE limits confirmation bias via its comprehensive origins from general scientific consensus.

Admissibility of Expert Testimony

Along these lines, the expert testimony provided during proceedings should also be supported by evidence. Multiple instances might impair an expert testimony claim, thus limiting its admissibility in court. For example, practitioners are expected to provide testimony that is supported by evidence in the field and not information that was developed for the sole purpose of being presented in court (*Daubert v. Merrell Dow Pharmaceuticals*, 1993). This type of testimony then is only based on an uninformed opinion that cannot be corroborated via scientific research. Another example to consider is those under criminal profiling. Several multiple techniques that are employed to develop such profiles, such as making use of a forensic report and extensive crime scene behavioral analysis. Yet, the information used for profiling is only as admissible as the techniques and tools used during the criminal investigation. For instance, if a piece of evidence is found to be compromised, then the profile should be adequately revised prior to expert testimony.

Historical Case Descriptions

Some individuals would argue that the direction of legal proceedings involving forensic psychology begins with the practitioner and ends in the contributions of a case. However, this process could be considered in reverse as cases could impact how forensic practitioners execute their duties in a court of law. Some cases could be examined that have influenced the relationship between forensic psychologists and the legal system. The first case to consider is that of Jason Daubert and Eric Schuller against Merrell Dow Pharmaceuticals (MDP). In was presented that a specific medication had resulted in congenital disabilities of the individuals after it was used during their early gestation periods (*Daubert v. Merrell Dow Pharmaceuticals Inc.*, 1993). However, the pharmaceutical company contended that the data that was originally presented by the plaintiffs was flawed. MDP argued that the data conclusions about the medication were not part of the scientific consensus and that its data did not pertain to life gestation, but instead, controlled gestation trials (*Daubert v. Merrell Dow Pharmaceuticals Inc.*, 1993). The second case to examine is that presented by the appellant Gonzalo Gonzales, and the people of the state of New York. It was noted that the juror's asked for a clarification of server legal terms and instructions that were presented for the initial of controlled substance charge once a supplemental charge was also included (*People v. Gonzales*, 1980). However, the Justice denied such request given that is was concluded that such earlier explanations were initially satisfactorily for the culmination of the trial (*People v. Gonzales*, 1980).

Impacts of the Cases

Each case of these cases might have contributed to the field of forensic psychology in the courts. The issues contended and their resolutions provide significant impacts as to a practitioner's data collection and use and juror examination. Upon Daubert's judgment, it was noted that expert testimony should be based on a two-fold standard. First, the expert's opinion should stem from a scientific view and method, as well as be informed by such data (Melton, Petrila, Poythress, & Slobogin, 2007). Furthermore, the case also noted that the individual should make use of data that directly informs the case at hand (*Daubert v. Merrell Dow Pharmaceuticals Inc.*, 1993). As such, the impacts towards forensic practitioners include a rigorous standard that might not be based on opposing testimonies of the plaintiff and defendant's opposing testimonies (Shuman & Sales, 1999). Instead, the standard would have to be by scientific evidence as proposed by peers in the field (Shuman & Sales, 1999). Lastly, the impacts of the case of Gonzales could be framed under a forensic practitioner's roles during early stages of the trial. For instance, it was concluded that the jurors should have the ultimate decision as to which pieces of information require further explanations during a trial (*People v. Gonzales*, 1980). Later, this case provided significant focus on literature and gap addressing as jurors had difficulties in understanding the legal and scientific terminology (*People v. Gonzales*, 1980). Consequently, this pertinent limitation was recognized by multiple states; and the comprehension of such terms and legal instructions is a key element for juror selection as conducted by practitioners (Haney, 1993).

Correctional Psychology

Major Roles

In addition to the variety of subspecialties discussed above, the correctional psychology area encompasses several essential roles. Forensic practitioners perform tasks such as assessing individuals upon facility reception for program placement (Bartol & Bartol, 2012). Here, a practitioner might provide assessments and evaluations to select programs that might best serve the needs of the reporting party and the inmate. Another relevant role to discuss is that of providing psychological treatment (González-Sala et al., 2017).

Forensic psychologists could provide both group and individual therapy and specialized treatment, such as that of sex offenders (Bartol & Bartol, 2012). Like with the case of police forensic psychology, practitioners could engage in recruitment and program development for correctional officers (Bartol & Bartol, 2012).

Major Responsibilities

Along with the crucial roles forensic psychologists have in the correctional arena, there are also important responsibilities that accompany such tasks. Perhaps a significant responsibility to note is that mentioned in the practitioner's guidelines. These include the stance of demonstrating integrity amongst the vast roles that forensic practitioners execute (American Psychological Association, 2016b). It could be argued that this responsibility is important as it allows for proper examination due to the inclusion of unbiased information (American Psychological Association, 2016a). For example, unbiased information based on the practitioner's adherence to integrity might lead to changes in the services that are provided in the facility (Brodsky, 2007). As a result, inmates are potentially able to receive purposeful treatment (Brodsky, 2007). Another responsibility to include is the need for psychologists to become aware of laws and other types of regulations that might impact their roles in the correctional environment (American Psychological Association, 2016b). For instance, each state might have a particular law that pertains to an inmate's release. These conditions could include a plan to access treatment and resources that might be developed by a practitioner (Wormith et al., 2007). Consequently, the role-responsibility relationship is relevant for all parties involved throughout the correctional process.

Psychologists in a Correctional Setting

Forensic psychologists working under the correctional subspecialty might engage in a wide variety of roles, thus providing support for the necessity of such practitioners in this setting. These roles could extend from initial inmate reception, throughout the sentencing servicing, and to develop plans upon release. In this regard, a significant role to consider is that involving mental health programs. Despite the apparent inherent task of providing such service, a more dilemmatic role is proposed in this text. Forensic psychologists could be expected to perform program evaluations from the reporting party's stance, but serve the inmate client. In a historical view, the role as program evaluator has been presented with multiple oppositions, some of which might culminate in the practitioner's livelihood (Brodsky, 2007). However, the importance of adequately executing this role relies both on the ethical, (American Psychological Association, 2016b) and legal (FindLaw, 2013) foundations. For instance, practitioners are expected to confine and provide adequate mental health services to inmates (FindLaw, 2013); a role to be jeopardized if a significantly faulty program is already emplace. Another relevant role to consider is that of researchers within the institutions.

It has been noted that research stemming from the forensic psychologist and originating from the correctional setting is an important element concerning treatment efficacy (Wormith et al., 2007). Researchers suggest that forensic practitioners might be able to develop natural observations of treatment that might not be otherwise available for other researchers outside of the setting (Wormith et al., 2007). Additionally, it could be argued that the importance of research is based on its potential of serving as a mean for advocacy (IACFP, 2010).

Correctional Psychology Challenges

Rights and Ethical Treatment of Inmates

Offenders, similar to law-abiding citizens, are entitled to legal protections. Likewise, it is also significant for forensic psychology professionals working in a correctional setting to acknowledge such protections. However, certain rights pertaining specifically to this population might be opposed to given their at-risk population status. Inmates have been granted legal rights such as those involving punishment or treatment that infringes on their dignity (FindLaw, 2013). This statement is in accordance with the Ethical Practice Guidelines as presented by the International Association for Correctional and Forensic Psychology (IACFP), formally known as the American Association for Correctional and Forensic Psychology (AACFP). One of the major propositions of the ethical practice in a correctional subspecialty is addressing the offenders in a dignified manner (IACFP, 2010). Another important right for offenders is access to medical treatment (FindLaw, 2013), which must be based on ethical and legal parameters of healthcare practices (IACFP, 2010). These ethical guidelines might be influenced given the practitioner's reporting party identification (American Psychological Association, 2016b) and by the offender's right to refuse such treatment (Bartol & Bartol, 2012). Lastly, regarding mental health protections, offenders that have not experienced physical harm cannot allege other psychological or emotional illness based on such injury (FindLaw, 2013). More often than not, it could be argued that ensuring such treatment is not upheld in certain correctional facilities and circumstances.

Justification

Regarding the offender's rights, perhaps the most encompassing and agreeable legal protection is that of being treated with dignity. It could be argued that this aspect is the most significant matter when addressing clients, regardless of their criminal record status. The rights including medical treatment have not gone unnoticed regarding debatable positions. First, access to standard medical care was turned down in a Supreme Court decision where a basic lower back imagery request was not granted to the offender (Bartol & Bartol, 2012). Secondly, the rights stipulating medical services were described as "adequate" but fail to include what this descriptor entailed for the offender's treatment (Bartol & Bartol, 2012). However, such treatment might also be impaired when considering psychological practices since many correctional facilities might lack the resources to address the demands of such institutions (IACFP, 2010). This issue stands in contradiction to specialty guidelines, as practitioners are only to perform duties for which they were trained (American Psychological Association, 2016b) and were initially agreed upon by the reporting party and consenting offender (IACFP, 2010). The third issue regarding such care is who the client is, which in the case of corrections, may not be the offender (IACFP, 2010). As such, practitioners must ensure that this distinction is carefully noted verbally and in writing (American Psychological Association, 2016b). Lastly, it could be contended that, if a psychological issue is deemed significant, offenders should be able to claim psychological harm.

Ethical Dilemmas

Since practitioners in this subspecialty are serving a vulnerable population, several ethical concerns should be evaluated. The population's practitioners could be engaged in a correctional setting have had many rights restricted given their current civil or criminal offender status (Allan, 2013). Consequently, a psychologist might be prone to extrapolate this type of specific rights restrictions to a far-reaching right negation. Therefore, a psychologist should be aware of the protections inmates have the right to receive. Likewise, forensic psychologists might be inherently exposed to different professional and ethical approaches; provided by their interactions with correctional officers and staff. As a result, practitioners might make use of ethical avenues of approach from other disciplines that might differ from those recommended by a forensic, ethical standard (Allan, 2013). Therefore, a potential way to address this concern is by utilizing ethical standards that pertain to one's discipline as means to not deter from the field's understanding of ethical conduct as well as any subspecialty codes.

Chapter 6: Criminal Forensic Psychology Writing

Criminal Case Reports

It could be argued that one of the areas in which forensic practitioners are frequently needed and manifested is in criminal court. Forensic practitioners could be summoned to conduct an evaluation of competency to consent to a search or seizure. This type is set to examine if an individual was exposed to a form of coercion when consenting procedures conducted by law enforcement (Melton, Petrila, Poythress, & Slobogin, 2007). Another evaluation to consider is that of the individual's competency to stand trial. Contrary to the admissibility of evidence, at its essence, this type of evaluation is centered in assessing the examinees' capacity to assist in their trial that might not be diminished by psychological impairment (Cox & Zapf, 2004). Lastly, another instance to include is that of competency to be sentenced. This particular evaluation could ask of a practitioner's expert opinion about the rehabilitation of a defendant whose conviction might include such treatment (Melton et al., 2007). In this sense, when compared with the previous evaluations, all three place a significant emphasis on the individual's degrees of psychological states.

Evaluation and Insights

The appropriateness of conducting the previous evolutions could be significantly supported by the time in which these evaluations are conducted. Within this area, each stage of the criminal process, prior, during, and sentencing also serves as contexts for evaluations. For instance, an evaluation of competency to consent to a search or seizure could be necessary during the deliberation of admitting the evidence. Further, the examination of confessions as collateral information (Giorgi-Guarnieri et al., 2002), might also lead to the evaluation concerning the potentiality of coercion. Another stage where forensic psychology practices can take place is during the defendant's trial. Before such event can take place, the defense or other legal parties might request an evaluation competency to stand trial. However, another instance in which this evaluation can take place is upon the verdict (Cox & Zapf, 2004). The type of sentencing might also be a source justification for evaluations. For instance, jurisdictions that impart capital punishment towards convicts, also by the same token, do not impose such penalty to those who are not found psychologically competent (Zapf, Boccaccini, & Brodsky, 2003).

Impact of Forensic Assessments

As means to comprehend the forensic risk assessment process and the impacts, such evaluation entails, students were given a case study to analyze. In this case, "Mr. H's" defense requested an evaluation to ascertain if a previous experienced sexual assault had a direct bearing on the indecent exposure charges (de Ruiter & Kaser-Boyd, 2015). Often, practitioners are summoned into the legal setting to address the specific question in order to assist in the adjudicative process (McLaughlin & Kan, 2014). Here, the forensic psychologist's roles included the selection, application, and interpretation of risk assessment and other instruments. Indeed, making use of such assorted sources of data could be used to compare the claims of the defendant during the interview process (Weiner & Otto, 2013). The practitioner made use of previous criminal, family, clinical history. In this regard, Mr. H's criminal history showed convictions for assault against his mother and carjacking (de Ruiter & Kaser-Boyd, 2015). However, the practitioner contended these offenses were conducted during the manic stages of Mr. H's Bipolar Disorder (BD) (de Ruiter & Kaser-Boyd, 2015). While serving his sentencing, Mr. H accused another inmate of rape while also exposing himself to female correctional officers. Upon imprisonment release, Mr. H was charged with attempted rape of a male and indecent exposure towards females (de Ruiter & Kaser-Boyd, 2015). Further, as substantiated by family and clinical history, Mr. H appeared to demonstrate symptoms consistent with BD and other psychotic symptoms; which he claimed commanded the genital exposure (de Ruiter & Kaser-Boyd, 2015). Lastly, the forensic psychologist collected data from standardized instruments to address the referral question.

Assessment Characteristics and Implications

The forensic psychologist responsible for the evaluations noted specific reasons that led to the selection of the instruments used for this case. For instance, the practitioner stated that such broad evaluations had to be completed in a limited amount of time (de Ruiter & Kaser-Boyd, 2015). As such, the Personality Assessment Inventory (PAI), the Psychopathic Personality Inventory-Revised (PPI-R), Static 99, and the Rapid Risk Assessment for Sex Offense Recidivism (RRASOR) were selected due to their brief administration periods. Additionally, as stated by the psychologist, another characteristic of the assessments was that the instrument provided a general and specific picture of characteristics that are consistent with symptomatic expression, willingness for treatment, and potential referrals (de Ruiter & Kaser-Boyd, 2015). For instance, the PAI could be used to determine Mr. H's scores clinically significant traits of aggression and APD; clinical data that is particularly noteworthy when addressing forensic questions (McLaughlin & Kan, 2014). The PPI-R could be effective in this case, given the defendant's psychotic history before the offense; which is an instrumental need for adequate forensic assessment (McLaughlin & Kan, 2014). A key element of the instruments' selection is the potential impacts regarding the outcome of the case. For example, the conjecture of the data stemming from the PAI and the PPI-R could be used to determine if the symptomatic expression could have resulted in the direct crime commission (de Ruiter & Kaser-Boyd, 2015), thus impacting matters of competency (McLaughlin & Kan,

2014). Lastly, the outcome of the case could have been influenced (RRASOR) since instruments concerning risk assessment provide data such as potential dangerousness, re-offenses (McLaughlin & Kan, 2014) and if there are in fact specific circumstances that led to the illegal behavior (Weiner & Otto, 2013). These three factors could result in treatment recommendations and the legal staff decisions for competency, mitigation, and sentencing.

Psychopathy Assessment

Psychopathy Checklist, Revised (PCL-R)

It could be argued that both laypersons and forensic psychologists describe behaviors as they leave from a particular norm. Consequently, the characteristics that a person might have that are distant from an observed average are used to describe unusual behavior. Such is the contention presented in the television documentary *The Psychopath Next Door* written by Jeremy Torrie. Here, a series of traits are shown as assessed by the standardized measure of Psychopathy Checklist, Revised (PCL-R). Its proponent and developer, Dr. Robert Hare, notes that sample used was from the Canadian prison population where psychopathy was perceived as prevalent (Torrie, 2014). The PCL-R examines 20 personality traits that have been found to be more prevailing amongst persons with psychopathy (Torrie, 2014). The assessment measure response ranges from 0 - 40, where the non-psychopathic population scores range from 0 -1 and the psychopathic cut off score is above 30 (Torrie, 2014). These traits include a lack of remorse, guilty or emphatic notions, shallow behavior, and egocentrism (Torrie, 2014). Despite that these personality traits commonly present in persons experiencing psychopathy, such traits are not perceived by the individual as malign or hurtful, but rather, a way to exploit and have personal gains (Torrie, 2014). It must be noted that these persons have a perception of reality and comprehend the concepts of "right" or "wrong" (Torrie, 2014).

Potential Risk Factors

Hare (2016) proposes that the factors of interpersonal, affective, lifestyle, and antisocial traits serve as means to understand the origin of psychopathy; thus determining forensic risk factors to predict future behavior. However, a potential risk factor that should be addressed by forensic psychology professionals is evidence consistent with the antisocial factor. For example, it has been shown that including the antisocial factor increases the fit for the four-factor regression model towards psychopathy in an offender population (Hare, 2016). Another to consider was that of criminal history regarding that of violent crime attempts or fulfilled violent offenses. There was a statically significant difference between 370 persons who met the psychopathy threshold and their likeliness of having a record of violent crime history versus non-psychopathic offenders (Storey et al., 2016). It must be stated that sole statistical findings do not provide a complete or ultimate foundation when addressing the future risk of an examinee (Vitacco et al., 2012). As such, risk factor evaluations should be considered as a dynamic rather than passive form of assessment on an individual basis (Vitacco et al., 2012).

Death Penalty

Assessments in a forensic psychology setting could be incorporated in quite significant processes such as those involving the death penalty. When these types of services are provided, professional psychological associations and national advocacy groups have voiced that such punishment should be reserved for persons who have less-than severe psychological illnesses (Death Penalty Information Center, 2017). The impacts of a forensic risk assessment extend beyond the inmate under examination, but also the community at large. As a result, one could consider how literature findings might inform the risk assessment, and thus, the inmate and society. It has been proposed that some of the literature that covers risks of an offender might be based on unverifiable assumptions (Nagin, 2014). For instance, risk assessment could include factors such as the potentiality of recidivism. However, some scholars argue making use of the previous history of crime frequency is perhaps a faulty mean to address risk (Nagin, 2014). This type of shortcoming could result in the diminished ability to conduct a proper assessment for the examinee. Further, the quality of an expert witness' testimony is based upon the ability to rely on scientific information and its emergent judgment (28 U.S.C. § 2072, 2014). However, if such requirements are not met, an apparent disservice to the judicial process and the public is done due to a substandard application of one's professional knowledge.

Guidelines and Death Penalty

To diminish or mitigate factors that could impair a forensic practitioner's work during a death penalty proceeding, a careful review of ethical guidelines could be warranted. One of the fundamental principles of the psychological field is that of taking measures to do no harm (American Psychological Association, 2017b). There are multiple means through which ethical violations that could particularly pertain to a practitioner's contributions and the death penalty. Cases where the examiner might be familiar with the victims or where the defendant appears to show no remorse might elicit examiner bias. This form of inclination is in direct opposition of impartiality that forensic examiners are ethically compelled to hold (American Psychological Association, 2016b). This type of bias could result in negative application, interpretation, and presentation of data; which is along the lines of causing harm. Other groups of defendants, such as juveniles, should be considered when evaluating capital punishment. For example, research suggests that the general public is less willing to deem the death penalty as a suitable punishment for a juvenile defendant than an adult (Vogel & Vogel, 2003). Consequently, this finding suggests a potential connection between capital punishment assessments involving a minor and society at large.

Instrument Appropriateness

Case Summary

As means to consider the significant features of psychometrics and their impacts throughout the assessment process, I will present the case study of "Kim." The Dutch female, age 22, was charged with murder and manslaughter. After law enforcement arrived at Kim's residence responding to an emergency call; she was taken into custody (de Ruiter & Kaser-Boyd, 2015). On the scene, the officers found the two lifeless bodies of two minors under the age of two, who have suffered fatal stabbing injuries (de Ruiter & Kaser-Boyd, 2015). The first responders reported that Kim appeared to be under the influence of a substance, that she had a scratch on her neck and traces of blood on her clothing (de Ruiter & Kaser-Boyd, 2015). The female contested the charges, stating that a male had committed the crime after she sustained a blow to the head (de Ruiter & Kaser-Boyd, 2015). A forensic psychologist was tasked to conduct a second examination of Kim's psychological state. This second examination arose given the judge's discontent with the first evaluation conducted by the Department of Justice of the Netherlands (de Ruiter & Kaser-Boyd, 2015).

Tool Appropriateness

This case's forensic practitioner chose the Minnesota Multiphasic Personality Inventory-2 (MMPI-2) among other data collection means to answer referral questions from the Dutch judicial system (de Ruiter & Kaser-Boyd, 2015). These referral questions included matters of diagnosis, competency, recidivism, comorbidity, and potential for treatment (de Ruiter & Kaser-Boyd, 2015). The MMPI-2 was developed as a broad and encompassing instrument with the purpose of identifying personality patterns and mental health illnesses (Butcher et al., 2001). The examinee's history along with the referral questions provided support regarding the forensic assessment instrument used in the case. For instance, according to the examiner, the data collected from the MMPI-2 provided support to broadly address the first four referral questions, thus providing a diagnosis for Post Traumatic Stress Disorder (PTSD) and depression. Yet, neither the data collected nor Kim's statements seem to substantiate the appropriateness of using this instrument since the examinee did not admit the crime when first evaluated. Lastly, the data regarding substance abuse and its potential for treatment provided support for this instrument's inclusion.

Instrument Evaluation

However, it could be argued that the reliability, validity, and the norming sample populations used for the instrument might oppose this view. The MMPI-2's Restructured Clinical (RC) Scales were employed by the examiner to address the potential diagnosis that pertained to the referral questions. The RC scales show a moderate inter-correlation with the content scales with a male and female sample (Nichols, 2011). Some researchers have argued that this significant relationship could show the RC's reduced validity to measure clinical symptoms (Nichols, 2011). Indeed, this validity limitation was found when a known population that might commonly experience psychological concerns, such as the 2000 prisoners that reported a lower score considerably under the clinically significant value for the MMPI-2 (Nichols, 2011). It could be argued that the reliability information for the RC might limit Kim's interpretation of clinically significant data as this might be impacted by under-sensitivity with females and clinical groups. Additionally, another limitation might be the norming sample used for the instrument. The developers noted that the participants utilized for the re-standardization of the second version were a non-correspondent sample of 2600 persons from a US-based population (Butcher et al., 2001). Therefore, the ethnic and national origin of Kim was not in accordance with the MMPI-2's North American norming population.

Understanding for Future Practice

The instrument assessment regarding this tool's use in the examinee's case study provides insights into the roles of a forensic psychologist. First, understanding the psychometrics to any given instrument prior to when a practitioner intends to use it provides an initial frame as to determine if the instrument will be a good selection for the referral questions. Further, these characteristics might also allow comprehending if the instrument could be a "good fit" for the examinee. As described earlier, these characteristics were contested since the instrument does not appear to be comprehensively aligned with this case study. Additionally, another significant factor to consider is how the forensic practitioner made use of the MMPI-2's data to extend the initial referral questions. The examinee was presented by law enforcement with non-substantiated evidence, which might lead a suspect into a false confession (Perillo & Kassin, 2011). The practitioner used the instrument's scales to draw conclusions and provide expert testimony as to either Kim's clinically significant symptom's might have made her prone to such type of confession (de Ruiter & Kaser-Boyd, 2015). It could be argued that this action might have overstated the instrument's proposed construct validity of clinical characteristics. Moreover, this conclusion extended beyond the client's referral question requests.

Substandard Reporting

Risks

Legal staff, and consequently, the general public, might place a level of trust regarding forensic assessments. This confidence could be based on the expected degree of accuracy that is demonstrated with adequate assessment reporting by forensic professionals. However, when such results are not reported accurately, there are some risks that could arise. First, adequate assessment should be considered within the limits of one's knowledge and the shortcomings of the evaluation itself (Weiner & Otto, 2013). Ergo, reporting inadequate results could include not stating one's experience and competency regarding the assessment process and the psychometric properties that might have limited interpretations. As a result, a risk could be providing expert witness testimony that was fundamentally faulty. Secondly, another risk to consider is the underestimation of assessment reporting regarding court impacts (de Ruiter & Kaser-Boyd, 2015). Despite that court decisions are not directly based on a forensic professional's work, such data presentation could be hindered and inadequately presented if the practitioner has a significant bias (de Ruiter & Kaser-Boyd, 2015). Therefore, a potential risk would be misinforming all legal parties. It must be noted that reporting results accurately rests upon the examiner's responsibility regardless of which methods were used for assessment (American Psychological Association, 2017b).

Ethical Guideline Violations

Along the lines of responsibilities of forensic professionals, other concerns are those that include breaches of confidentiality. These ethical and legal violations could be arguably exacerbated when an exciting and high profile is at hand. For instance, a particular example of such breach could be social media commentary. Although these comments could be provided privately, providing information outside of the context that it was originally intended for (American Psychological Association, 2017b) could result in an ethical violation. Furthermore, another ethical consideration with such cases is breaching confidentiality through publications. For instance, forensic professionals might feel inclined to develop a case study or another type of release to document such exciting or well-known case. Yet, this type of work might require inherently cautionary steps to limit confidentiality concerns, including the parties' consent (American Psychological Association, 2017b). Finally, referrals that are unique might potentially hinder the professional's judgment due to its rare and uncommon characteristics. Ethical considerations are warranted such as recognizing biases throughout the entire assessment process (American Psychological Association, 2016b).

Juvenile Crime and Adult Trials

Crime accusation might elicit emotional responses and spark the interest of laypersons and forensic professionals alike. However, it could be argued that severe or violent crimes committed by juveniles might persuade the general population (Greene & Evelo, 2013) in requesting that such persons should be tried as adults. Therefore, instrument appropriateness is crucial for these particular instances. Severe crimes include those that have resulted in the murder of an individual during the property crime of carjacking (18 U.S.C. of 1992 § 2119, 1996). The first case study example includes a 17-year-old accused with the murder of a minor 6 years of age. The male had a previous history regarding an armed robbery. Along with two other defendants, the 17-year-old suspect was charged with violently stealing a vehicle occupied by the child's mother. The 6-year-old victim showed multiple gunshot wounds resulting in the child's death. Another severe crime is that of killing a state correctional officer (18 U.S.C. of 1994 § 1121, 1996). The second case study example includes such charges. Here, a 15-year-old juvenile inmate was accused of killing a correctional officer after she walked in into his cell. The correctional officer's strangulation spanned over the course of several minutes; later resulting in her death. The correctional facility's security cameras recorded this criminal offense. The prosecutors', the victims' relatives, and the general publics' opinion held that, in both cases, the 17-year-old and 15-year-old should be tried in adult courts.

Developmental Criteria

Despite the fact that some individuals might deem this change of court as necessary, there are developmental factors that could be legally required for a juvenile to be tried as an adult. It has been proposed that young persons might not yet have undergone physiological, social, and psychological processes that might assist in the individual's judgment (Greene & Evelo, 2013). First, research provides evidence that young individuals' frontal lobe development has not yet culminated until the first half of their 20's (National Conference of State Legislatures, n.d.). In turn, this developmental stage could result in a substandard capacity to conduct adequate judgment and proneness to impulsivity (National Conference of State Legislatures, n.d.). Along these lines, the yet underdeveloped social development might make young individuals more predisposed to social pressures stemming from their peers (The John D. and Catherine T. MacArthur Foundation, 2006). Lastly, limited psychological development also provides a potential foundation for careless behavior (Greene & Evelo, 2013). Given these significant factors, forensic psychology professionals might be called upon to assess how these factors might limit the minor's competency given developmental immaturity. Another role could include that of conducting risk assessments to address the potential of re-offending as a juvenile or later as an adult.

Chapter 7: Courtroom Testimony

Testifying

In some cases, the nature and elements of the case could pose a significant challenge for practitioners that provide expert testimony. Specifically, cases that pertain to capital offenses and the severely mentally ill could be examples of such demands. Such cases could involve psychological issues. One example to consider is that of Andrew Goldstein. In the turn of the millennia, Goldstein was accused of the murder of a female by shoving the female into an oncoming New York subway train (Rohde, 1999). It was noted that Goldstein had failed to take anti-psychotic medication (*People v. Goldstein*, 2004) later becoming erratic immediately prior to the offense, which had alerted witnesses (*People v. Goldstein*, 2004). Furthermore, Goldstein had an extensive history of schizophrenia (*People v. Goldstein,* 2004), but an insanity defense was denied due to the expert witness' testimony. The forensic practitioner noted that psychotic episodes are not momentary in nature (Rohde, 1999), despite not having examined the client's psychotic episode history (*People v. Goldstein*, 2004). Upon a first mistrial, the court convicted Goldstein of second-degree murder since he was aware that his action was wrong, thus not satisfying the state's criteria for insanity defense (*People v. Goldstein*, 2004).

Offering Expert Testimony

Despite the fact that there were other developments, in this case, its origins warrant further considerations as it pertains to providing expert witness testimony. First, one factor to consider is a practitioner's summoning provided a subpoena. In this regard, it is imperative that the professional includes and presents information that directly pertains to the case; such as Goldstein's history of schizophrenia. This step should be taken as practitioners have an ethical responsibility to limit the amount of information that can mischaracterize an individual (Melton, Petrila, Poythress, & Slobogin, 2007). Another step to engage in is the preliminary preparation for the deposition. Here, a practitioner should carefully develop reports that clearly present the referral questions at hand (Melton et al., 2007). This step appears to have been overlooked in Goldstein's case as it was admitted by the expert witness that no recorded reviews were conducted nor included in his report's conclusions (Rohde, 1999). This issue aligns with another step: preparation for the testimony. The credibility of the witness is one of the utmost focus points during trials (Babitsky & Mangraviti, 2000). As a result, it is relevant that practitioners account for cross-examination difficulties. A way to mitigate issues during this step is to meet with the legal parties; such as the attorneys (Babitsky & Mangraviti, 2000). During the appellation, this shortcoming was noted from the defense's end (_People v. Goldstein_, 2004). This step could be used to examine the inquiries that might take place during the forensic practitioner's role as an expert witness (Babitsky & Mangraviti, 2000).

Courtroom Presence

Expert witness testimony relies on one's capability to express scientifically sound opinions about the case. Arguably, just as relevant is how such testimony is portrayed to the jury. These observations are facilitated given that expert testimony most often is accompanied by both emotional and physical expressions of the speaker (Brodsky, 2004). Undoubtedly, both of these factors could play a role in how the testimony is received and vindicated. Previously recorded testimonies could assist in observing such underlying factors of communication strategies. These strategies can be observed in both of the upcoming criminal and civil proceeding examples. First, consider a civil trial that involves the deliberation as to whether or not the visitation rights of a father should be terminated. An expert would need to demonstrate indications of powerful speech. For example, practitioners should appear comfortable with explaining their roles during the psychosexual assessment of the father. This rationale is based on a perceived sense of familiar tone and speech, which is generally considered an adequate mean to represent oneself as credible (Brodsky, 2004). Likewise, a practitioner should appear to have extensive knowledge of such assessment by providing a breakdown of its purpose, procedure, conclusions, and general recommendations to the court and his admission to possible limitations of the process.

Now consider the scenario of a second practitioner and a case concerning a capital offense. At first glance, it could be mentioned that style of dress of the expert witness should always be appropriate for the setting and the manners being handled via formal attire. This practitioner should demonstrate adequate reflections based on careful and accurate listening. During the cross-examination process, an expert could expect to be examined multiple times regarding the nature of receiving compensation for his work. Such questions could be paraphrased on numerous occasions as means to perhaps elicit some confusion. However, a technique that this second expert could employ is active listening as means to identify such strategy. The use of such techniques is not uncommon, as attorneys might purposely use such conversation to favor their clients (Boccaccini, 2002).

Impacts towards Forensic Practitioners

Each of the communication strategies identified in both the civil and criminal trials might serve as contributors or examples of effective courtroom communication. First, expert witness testimony is considered one of the most significant factors of trials, as the majority of the information comes from said sources among other forms of testimony (Boccaccini, 2002). As such, forensic practitioners might make use of training before testifying (Boccaccini, Gordon, & Brodsky, 2005), to attain powerful speech. Without such speech, carefully developed assessments and opinions could be lost. Style of dress and other forms of appearance (Brodsky, 2004) provide an initial superficial understanding of the formality of the individual. This type of message could portray, from the witness to the jury, recognition of the severity of all matters addressed in a legal setting. Lastly, active listening facilitates the identification of techniques that might be used to misrepresent (Babitsky & Mangraviti, 2002), and perhaps hinder, a scientifically-based testimony.

Problems as an Expert Witness

Case Study

Multiple cases capture the attention of both forensic psychology professionals and the general public. Due to its characteristics, the involvement of mental illness symptoms and type of offense, Andrew Goldstein's case had such drawing. Goldstein was accused of tossing a woman, without provocation, into a subway track of New York (*People v. Goldstein*, 2004). It was agreed by the defense and prosecution's forensic witnesses that Goldstein had a significant history of severe schizophrenia, outbursts of psychotic symptoms (*People v. Goldstein*, 2004), and that he had not taken medication to subside these issues immediately before the alleged attack (*People v. Goldstein*, 2004). Upon impact, the female died of her injuries, and Goldstein was found guilty of second-degree murder (*People v. Goldstein*, 2004). The prosecution noted that the offense was carried out provided the defendant's sexual frustration with women and not his mental illness (*People v. Goldstein*, 2005). In this text, however, it will be assumed that the data sources used for the case included instruments such as Wechsler Adult Intelligence Scale-III, the MMPI-2, Psychopathy

Checklist and the Rorschach. Other provided sources of information were from the FBI's behavioral analysis unit, which developed a profile, and opposing attorneys. Despite that, the information on commonly known mental illnesses might not necessarily be misunderstood by the jurors and the general public (Mark, 1999), it is imperative to prepare for potential challenges.

Daubert Challenge

The Daubert standard might be an issue regarding these procedures since it was not demonstrated that the forensic practitioner had training and experience in administering and interpreting the tests. Mainly, it could be argued that the use of a projective test might not be aligned with the standard since it might not have general acceptance as a reliable method in the field (*Daubert v. Merrell Dow Pharmaceuticals*, 1993). This standard mentions that the foundations utilized to provide expert testimony should be developed through scientific procedures, and its conclusions are commonly accepted by peers in the field (*Daubert v. Merrell Dow Pharmaceuticals,* 1993). Another significant factor of the standard is that the scientifically based information used in a given case should be directly related to the proceeding (*Daubert v. Merrell Dow Pharmaceuticals*, 1993). A possible technique a practitioner might use for preparation for such challenge is directly addressing the inquiries of the data sources' origin (Babitsky & Mangraviti, 2000). It could be argued that since tow parties, the agency and opposing attorneys provided data, its conclusions might not necessarily serve and cater to a practitioner's report and findings. Further, one must also address and study the validity (Melton, Petrila, Poythress, & Slobogin, 2007) of the instruments carefully.

Cross-Examination Anticipation

Consultant Experience

During cross-examination, there are inquiries that one could anticipate similar to the following:

- _Question 1: Do you have extensive experience in administrating tests with an "X" population?_

Arguably, this type of question could be expected as an attorney might make use of techniques that are aimed at reducing the expert witness' credibility (Babitsky & Mangraviti, 2000). There are multiple ways in which a practitioner could prepare for a said line of questioning. First, practitioners could focus on not attempting to mischaracterize themselves concerning the amount of forensic psychology experience. Additionally, an expert witness should also attempt to prepare for such question by honestly portraying their experience outside of the courtroom. This technique limits the amount of information opposing counsel might attempt to utilize that might contradict the witness' experience statements during deposition (Babitsky & Mangraviti, 2000).

Psychometrist Experience

- *Question 2: Dr. Z, since the year "X," you have primarily worked as a therapist/supervisor/professor. Haven't you?*

In a similar fashion to the previous question, this inquiry is also set in discrediting the witness. However, in this case, the intent is to discredit the practitioner as means to demonstrate that the witness has not executed the role of a forensic psychology examiner. Since expert witnesses rely on their experience to provide testimony (Mark, 1999), attempting to minimize said experience in front of jurors could play a significant role in forwarding the attorney's case. As a result, a practitioner should prepare to testify by keeping a varied and relevant background concerning forensic psychology evaluations.

Instrument Validity

- *Question 3: The subscale "X" is used for addressing "Y" symptom/trait. Isn't it true that this subscale reflected a normal/abnormal result for Mr. "B"?*

It could be argued that this last question example could serve a myriad of purposes. For instance, this inquiry could be used to potentially assert that a particular portion of the test might not, in fact, reflect such use. Another use of this question could be not allowing the expert witness to explain neither what the subscale is used for nor the meaning of the results. Often, attorneys might attempt to question the sources of information (Poythress, 1980). Practitioners could prepare for this type of misinterpretation of the data used for the testimony by preparing a statement that adequately conveys its intent to the jury. This technique, in turn, could be achieved by meeting with counsel as to discuss and rehearse for questions that might arise (Brodsky, 2004).

Testimony Elements

Effective Testimony

It could be a logical conclusion that if one recalls an event as accurately as possible, then recalling behaviors involving a case should be a seemingly easy task. However, this is not the case in practice when faced with different forms of testimony. In a broad sense, it could be argued that certain testimonies might be more effective when cross-examined in a court of law. For instance, an example to consider is the witnesses of a juvenile defendant. In this case, an adolescent African American male was arrested and charged with the murder of a senior Caucasian female upon a failed burglary attempt (Le Goff, Poncet, & Jeanneau, 2001). Multiple individuals came forth as witnesses in the case, such as the defendant's sibling. In a particular instance, the prosecutor attempted to use a term that the witness had not, which the witness promptly denied using (Le Goff, Poncet, & Jeanneau, 2001). The lead detective did other effective testimony instances when confronted by credibility issues (Le Goff, Poncet, & Jeanneau, 2001); the witness did not attempt to avoid the questions nor argue with counsel. Lastly, when another detective was confronted with a potential conflict of interest within the department (Le Goff, Poncet, & Jeanneau, 2001), the detective appeared to keep a professional demeanor.

Effectiveness Elements

As noted previously, these statements could be used as examples of useful testimony provided each of their elements. For instance, it is common for opposing attorneys to make use of techniques that could misrepresent the statements provided by a witness (Melton, Petrila, Poythress, & Slobogin, 2007). The witness, in turn, identified such technique and corrected counsel without an elaborate explanation. This last characteristic resulted in the desired element, although counsel will not typically permit the witness to elaborate (Babitsky & Mangraviti, 2000). The second and third examples of effective testimony as provided by the first detective include how the detective directly answered questions that revealed limitations in his investigative work. This element is significant during testimony as it brings to light deficiencies in one's work in a procedure that could be employed by opposing attorneys (Babitsky & Mangraviti, 2000). Lastly, the second detective provided calm statements even though his professional capacity came into question. This element of carrying oneself in such a manner is indeed a sought after and crucial component for effective witness testimony (Babitsky & Mangraviti, 2000).

Communication

Perhaps one environment where ineffective communication should be avoided and critically damaging is in that of a legal arena. Effective and ineffective communication in the courtroom is then composed of several different characteristics on behalf of several parties; including expert witnesses and attorneys. One example of the latter is the ability of the expert witness not to provide opinions or inferences that do not extend beyond those that were informed by their training and experience. As means to ensure effective communication, persons should solely express opinions within the confines of their expertise (Babitsky & Mangraviti, 2000). Another significant key element of effective communication is that of ascertaining the intent of the dialogue (Wadsworth Cengage Learning, 2007). For example, during proceedings, the intent of the listener, such as the prosecution or defense attorney, might be focusing on statements from the expert with the intent of providing criticism to particular points (Wadsworth Cengage Learning, 2007). Therefore, the comments are perhaps being dismissed because only pre-determined phrases are being scanned during the conversation. Consequently, effective communication can mitigate this type of listening via goal identification. Conversely, ineffective communication consists of faults while executing roles as a speaker or a listener. One such example is that of reacting in an emotional manner when certain phrases are present (Wadsworth Cengage Learning, 2007). Along these lines, a professional bearing during communication proves to be a deterrent to distractions between the speaker and the listeners (Babitsky & Mangraviti, 2000).

Effective vs. Ineffective Communication

There are potential benefits of effective communication examples of expertise confinement and goal identification. On the other hand, there are possible consequences of ineffective communication stemming from emotional reactions or poor professional demeanor. For instance, remaining within one's area of expertise limits erroneous statements, which could result in the incorrect characterization of the speaker (Babitsky & Mangraviti, 2000). Goal identification then allows the listener to avoid responding to misleading statements that were specifically targeted at fallacious communication. Ineffective communications stemming from emotional reactions could result in the actual message being tainted with underlying tones of the speaker's mental state (Boccaccini, 2002). Therefore, the intended communication could be lost to an emotionally-based expression rather than by the statement being made. Similarly, a possible impact of lacking professional demeanor is that individuals are not able to focus on the message that is being expressed rather than marginal or unintended messages. This issue could result in interpretations of the person's character, thus affecting the speaker's credibility (Boccaccini, 2002).

Professionalism

Courtroom Etiquette

One of the key characteristics of professionalism is its implied adherence to a given standard as defined by those in the field. As such, when individuals drift away from the expectation of a profession, their commitment to their profession might be subject to questioning. Such instances can be evaluated within a courtroom setting. Here, legal as well as other individuals with extensive educational backgrounds could meet as means to address a particular case. Therefore, courtroom etiquette might become an essential component as to how a case develops. Forensic psychology professionals, in turn, might have to abide by the etiquette as it is expected in that area. A breach in courtroom etiquette to consider is the style of dress. Within a civil trail example, a psychological expert witness could provide his testimony in casual, summer attire. The trait of a presentable image has been argued to have had diminished considerably on those who take part in a legal arena (Flynn, 2000). Another breach in courtroom etiquette is that arguing rather than presenting a testimony. In a criminal trial example, a forensic psychology professional might argue with counsel, later demonstrating remarks of self-praise as a justification.

Consequences of Breaches

Not abiding by these, as well as other aspects of courtroom etiquette, could result in several consequences. These outcomes could be observed as they affect the individual, the testimony being offered, and in a more overreaching sense, the field. For instance, perhaps the most immediate outcome of substandard appearance is its potential to ruin the perception of the individual's image (Flynn, 2000). Moreover, it has been argued that when such conclusions are reached about a person, other individuals in the courtroom might question the quality or competence of the expert's work (Flynn, 2000). Furthermore, a poor image could result in an unimpressive impression (Kanemoto, 2005), and perhaps, by extension, individuals might not take an interest in the witness' testimony. The strategy of attempting to note weaknesses of a witness is a technique commonly employed by attorneys (Babitsky & Mangraviti, 2000). Arguably this technique might make experts prone to eliciting certain responses. A possible consequence of arguing and self-glorifying one's background is not portraying oneself as an expert. This action ultimately hinders the forensic psychology professional's role in the courtroom by appearing as an advocate (Babitsky & Mangraviti, 2000). Lastly, the lack of showing a humble persona might result in a diminished capacity to recognize errors, and thus, an inability to address shortcomings (Kanemoto, 2005).

Ethical Dilemmas and Challenges

The roles within investigative forensic psychology have been faced with much criticism and challenges. Primarily, these ethical and challenging concerns have been based both on the accuracy and the legitimacy of the inferences that were drawn. For example, some scholars argue that there could be a significant gap in the time frame between when the crime was committed to when the practitioner draws conclusions about the suspect (Haun, Gallagher, & Milz, 2010). Furthermore, another issue that has been presented is that of drawing inferences that extend far beyond what research, evidence, and criminal profiling suggests (Perri & Lichtenwald, 2009). Scholars propose that these issues could be mitigated via adherence to the investigation's evidence (Bartol & Bartol, 2012), and by immediate correction of statements once they have been opposed to by new or better criminal evidence (Allan, 2013).

Communication and Challenges

Forensic Assessment Communication

Despite the difficulties of child custody evaluations, forensic practitioners can reference ethical guidelines, particularly with high profile cases. For instance, effective communication of forensic assessment findings could be a significant factor in this process. An important consideration is maintaining a clear understanding of who is the reporting party of the assessment. Here, practitioners should note and maintain throughout the assessment and recommendation process, that the client is not the high-profile person, but the judicial system (Patel & Choate, 2014). This might assist individuals to focus on the referral duties and remain impartial. Further, practitioners should remain within the confines of the assessments' purpose, validity, and reliability when reporting results (American Psychological Association, 2016b). Lastly, practitioners must also acknowledge the confines of their roles as to avoid conflicts of interest (American Psychological Association, 2016b).

Ethical Dilemmas and Challenges

Forensic professionals working in this field could be confronted with several dilemmas that could be resolved. A significant problem to consider is within the expert witness role. Scholars have suggested that forensic practitioners might become prone to bias due to this role's frequency. On the one hand, a psychologist could become significantly attached and, on the other hand, become indifferent as testimonies become more numerous (Allan, 2013). This issue could possibly be mitigated via self-care. This approach might often be overlooked by psychologists in general. Yet, its potential benefits with health care professionals and psychologists alike could help by adequately approaching clients. A second issue to discuss is that of bias while working in a civil setting. Psychologists working in the assessment of juror qualifications might demonstrate researcher and interviewer bias. This form of pre-conceptualization could stem from prior interactions with similar individuals which the practitioner might be presently experiencing (Allan, 2013). It could be argued that this concern could be addressed with out-group familiarization. After this bias is recognized, practitioners could make proactive efforts to include research about the bias.

Controversial Issues

As with other fields of practice, psychologists in the civil subspecialty are not exempt from debated issues. For instance, some have suggested that assessment tool selection might be based on the case and not based on the instrument's validity *towards* the case (Arbach et al., 2017). Consequently, assessment inadequacy, competent evaluation, and possibly, examinee harm could arise from inappropriate instrument use and application. Secondly, even when assessments are conducted adequately, the conclusions could still be impaired. Roughly one in ten legal professionals note that the psychologists failed to provide proper foundations as to whether or not a mental illness impacted the alleged offense execution (Gianvanni & Sharman, 2017).

Chapter 8: Ethics in Forensic Psychology

General Ethical Issues

The factuality of information is arguably one of the most desirable traits when considering the preponderance of the evidence. There is a myriad of factors that could hinder the truthfulness or accuracy of such evidence; including ethical issues from forensic psychologists. Such ethical concerns could be the level of forensic knowledge of a practitioner and issues towards multicultural layers of diversity. In the case of the former, this ethical concern is clearly noted in ethical principles for forensic psychologists as well as similar professional fields that currently have a role in a forensic setting. These ethical guidelines state that persons executing such roles should possess a level of expertise for which they possess a significant level of experience about law and their respective fields (Melton, Petrila, Poythress, & Slobogin, 2007). Further, not only is this type of knowledge necessary, but should also comply with its professional standards of knowledge (Melton et al., 2007). As such, a potential concern in this area could be that of limited experience or training in a forensic role. In the case of multicultural concerns, diversity bias is similarly considered as yet another impairment of forensic judgment; regardless of intentionality (American Academy of Psychiatry and the Law, 2005). Additionally, it is recommended that psychologists evaluate the impact that their personal multicultural layers might have while exercising such roles within the profession (American Psychological Association,

2016b). For instance, such biases could include those of individually held religious beliefs.

Impacts in the Courts

The negative impacts of substandard experience and diversity bias are perhaps a living testimony of its detrimental effects. Undoubtedly, these issues impact forensic psychology. For example, one could evaluate the effects that could be providing while under a forensic evaluator role. It has been mentioned that forensic practitioners should pursue and aim towards providing quality services; including those given while being an evaluator (American Psychological Association, 2016b). However, such high standard cannot be achieved based on the lack of adequate training and expertise. Consequently, this fault could result in poor services as an evaluator, becoming then a provider of inadequate information in a court of law. Lastly, diversity bias that could stem from the practitioner's belief could result in harmful consequences to the parties involved in the proceeding. These issues could include abuse (American Academy of Psychiatry and the Law, 2005) and unfairness (American Psychological Association, 2017b) due to impaired judgment and forensic practice. Individuals are encouraged to make use of significant developments in the field, such as scientific consensus of data (Otto & Heilburn, 2002) as a potential moderator for this issue.

Technology

Good methods and fields should constantly build upon research and the experience of its professionals as they arise from the practitioners. The constant application of such techniques gives room for constant research expansion, fine-tuning, and the emergence of new assets to be used in the discipline. These are potential sources from which technologies have been derived from to be later included in the field of forensic psychology. A technology to discuss is that Discriminant Function Analysis (DFA). Among other uses, the long-standing field of forensic anthropology makes use of the DFA to assist in the identification of individuals whose remains are in a severe decomposition stage (Adebisi, 2009). This analysis uses characteristics that arise from the remains such as ethnic group origin and possible type of death to aid forensic examiners (Adebisi, 2009). The second technology to mention is video conferencing. Via this modus, individuals make use of cost-effective software and hardware where direct in-person consultation might not be readily available or viable (Miller, Clark, Veltkamp, Burton, & Swope, 2008). Lastly, Brain Fingerprinting technique involves the non-test use of electroencephalography ([EEG]; Littlefield, 2009). Here, P300 waves are measured after a stimulus is provided concerning details of a crime (Iacono, 2008). Later, if these waves are detected, it might be attributed to thoughts of fear (Littlefield, 2009) and, in other cases, the culpability of the subject (Iacono, 2008).

Impacts towards psychologists

Each of these technologies could be relevant to the courts if we also consider the roles of forensic psychologists. For example, the DFA as carried out by forensic anthropology requires extensive knowledge of physiology, bodily injuries, and ancestral DNA (Adebisi, 2009). This type of information could be somewhat of technical nature, thus affecting how members of the court receive that type of scientific information. As a result within their role of being a consultant for jury selection, it is relevant for the practitioner to take into consideration how to eliminate persons from sitting in a jury position that might not necessarily grasp this technology adequately for the case. Regarding the second technology of video conferencing, there could be an impact on the court as practitioners who become expert witnesses might be able to conduct meetings with counsel. Practitioners could engage in consultation roles with attorneys provided that other venues are limited. Consequently, the information that might be presented from both the attorney and the forensic psychology expert witness could be examined before meeting in court (Miller et al., 2008). In regards to Brain Fingerprinting, technique significantly impacts the courts if one considers the premise that defendants might be unknowingly stating a guilty stance of a crime (Iacono, 2008). Here, a question of the constitutional protection of self-incrimination could be considered (U.S. Const. amend. V.) as practitioners could be summoned to address the defendant's ability to confess.

Multiculturalism

Diversity and Forensic Psychology

Forensic practice, as the term suggests, could mainly be associated with roles involving legal settings. As such, this potentially conventional view of the field might limit a professional's perception of the diversified clientele and tasks within the forensic practice. Indeed, some researchers suggest a narrow view of general psychology and, ergo, forensic subspecialties have been historically focused on European-American cultures (Bartol & Bartol, 2012). Therefore, it could be argued that not considering multiculturalism with other non-European-American persons results in inadequate practice and substandard application of psychological knowledge. Multiculturalism could generally be referred to as the accountability of cultural diversity for effective practice (Bartol & Bartol, 2012). In other words, persons who may not particularly have social or cultural preponderance given gender, race, creed, sexual orientation, and other factors could warrant further attention in psychological practice. This perspective has been promoted in recent decades provided the increment in diverse populations in the United States and its apparent projected growth (Bartol & Bartol, 2012). As means to provide measures to address the inherent complexity present in multicultural considerations, various guidelines have been implemented for both psychologists and those specialized in the forensic field alike.

Important Guideless to Forensic Roles

The American Psychological Association (APA) (1990) developed the Guidelines for Providers of Psychological Services to Ethnic, Linguistic, and Culturally Diverse Populations as well as the Guidelines on multicultural education, training, research, practice, and organizational change for psychologists (2002) as a foundation for appropriate practice. When considering the roles of a forensic psychology professional within forensic psychology subspecialties, there are specific guidelines to evaluate. For example, the subfield of Police Psychology could entail the role of training personnel (Bartol & Bartol, 2012). Therefore, psychologists that engage in training should themselves become acquainted with the individuals they are currently servicing (American Psychological Association, 2002). Another important role, found within the subfield of victimology and victimology services, is addressing persons who have survived or witnessed crimes (Bartol & Bartol, 2012). Here, psychologists should present what such roles entail while considering the effect that person's cultural background might have in such practice (American Psychological Association, 1990). Lastly, a legal psychologist could be tasked with conducting research as means to sample a community and serve an attorney (Bartol & Bartol, 2012). Therefore the American Psychological Association (2002) notes that psychologists should become aware of specific multicultural differences between them, as researchers and the sample being addressed, as these views could ultimately mold behaviors and worldviews.

Relevancy of the Guideless

The varied roles forensic psychologists may have while engaging in practice might warrant significant familiarization with multicultural differences and general multicultural competency. As noted previously, each role, trainer, service person, and researcher calls for consideration of training outside the forensic specialization. Perhaps, more importantly, is the application of such skills and training as means to promote the growth and improvement of those whom they serve. Consequently, the incorporation of multiculturalism might impact the practice of forensic psychology by providing an encompassing view of the psychology-law intercept. Such inclusion then results in meeting the needs of diverse clients and legal staff professionals.

Differences and Biases

National Origin

Other than the records and the information gathered during the assessment process, practitioners should account for other factors that might impact the case. These elements could include those from the background of both the examiner and the examinee. For example, in a fundamental sense, psychologists are to consider within and out-group national origin differences that impact their work (American Psychological Association, 2003). As a result, when practitioners are evaluating defendants for testimony, psychologists should take into account potential cultural biases from a group of people, since stereotypical thinking might significantly impact evaluation processes (Shepherd, & Lewis-Fernández, 2016). For example, practitioners should make note that if they have some familiarization with persons from a specific nationality and not deem this information as final; as this knowledge should account for individual differences among national origin groups.

Gender

Other differences that should be considered are the potential gender differences during the evaluation process. The examination should account for two significant factors that could hinder the data collection process, data interpretation, and how the testimony is later provided to the court. First, forensic psychology evaluators should be able to determine if they currently possess any preconceived ideas that might impact how the examination is conducted. Additionally, an examiner should account for how said gender differences might impact the examinee's ability to develop rapport during the examination process. Therefore, accounting for these differences should be viewed, by the practitioner, from both parties.

Religious Background

Lastly, differences in religious backgrounds can prove to be a significant factor when conducting evaluations. For example, a practitioner should be able to exclude that the manifestation of symptoms revolves around a religious connotation or the expression of mental illness (American Psychiatric Association, 2013). Furthermore, practitioners should also consider if certain religious background characteristics are being used as a symptom in of itself. Previously, it has been noted that fundamentalist values were used in the late 20th century as diagnostic criteria to provide a diagnosis (Ortiz-Díaz, 2018). Overall, religious discrimination has, in turn, been found to be a significant contributing factor towards anxiety (Ortiz-Díaz, 2018). Provided these outcomes, forensic psychology practitioners should exert caution when conducting evaluations.

Assessment and Multicultural Differences

Given the cultural and national origin assortment present in Western countries, psychologists could undoubtedly be summoned to work with diverse clients. However, this task might imply an inherent use of ethical guidelines as means to better serve the clients and uphold the field's standards. To evaluate such process, I will present the case study of an adolescent immigrant female charged with first-degree murder given the act of neonaticide (de Ruiter, & Kaser-Boyd, 2015). The forensic practitioner was tasked to conduct a mental health assessment of Jane's state. The practitioner recognized a concern pertaining to instrument use and application since the examinee provided both an acculturation and language barrier issue (de Ruiter, & Kaser-Boyd, 2015). The psychologist refrained from using tools that have not been standardized nor could be used with an examinee; which might be in accordance with professional standards and diverse groups. Here, it is noted that the examinee should have a level of competency regarding the instrument's language (American Psychological Association, 1993). Another significant example of ethical guidance adherence in this case study's forensic psychology practitioner was recognizing her limitations concerning the examinee's cultural background. The psychologist made use of a cultural expert as means to assist in the interview and cultural-bound differences that might impact data interpretation (de Ruiter, & Kaser-Boyd, 2015). In this regard, practitioners should consider culturally-related factors that might influence how the examinee's data should be interpreted (American Psychological Association, 2017b).

Culture-Bound Syndrome Biases

It is imperative and a professional ethical responsibility to recognize how the practitioner's own multicultural background might result in biases when addressing clients (American Psychological Association, 1993). This case study presented two multicultural factors that might pose as a potential bias. These variables included the immigration status of the examinee and sex. Despite the fact that the practitioner might not be foreign-born, it might be often and mistakenly assumed that one's race is a synonym to national origin. This discriminatory exposure on the future practitioner's end might result in biases, and perhaps, unwarranted sympathy towards the client's current state based on immigration discrimination. Similarly, presenting oneself with a particular sex might result on "positive" biases towards a client of the same sex. However, this form of bias could result in a disservice to the client and current or future forensic psychology roles. As such, forensic psychologists are recommended to engage in consultation as means to minimize such biases and improve assessment accuracy (Varela & Conroy, 2012).

Ethical Conflict Scenario

Despite a forensic psychologist's training and professional experience, there could be instances that might prove to be problematic. This is the case of ethical conflicts and dilemmas that might not be easily resolved. For instance, the first ethical conflict to address is that involving possible dual roles. Here, a psychologist could be conducting an interview that might potentially result in the examinee experiencing distress. While facing this concern, the psychologist could perceive both a role as an examiner in a legal setting and as a clinician that might need to conduct a debriefing. The second ethical concern could be that of being considered for an expert whiteness function. In this case, the psychologist has some familiarization with the task at hand and might be considered an expert among peers, but might lack the necessary skills to fulfill the expert witness task adequately. In both conflicts, a psychologist could make use of ethical code/guidelines while facing such challenges.

Conflict Resolution

Psychologists and forensic psychology professionals alike experiencing the first conflict could reference the fourth specialty guideline forensic psychologists. In this regard, psychologists are to clearly establish and present their roles and what services and functions the parties should expect from the practitioner (American Psychological Association, 2016b). While describing their roles, a psychologist should consider the fifth guideline under the ethical principles for psychologists. In this context, a practitioner should avoid deceptive descriptions of the services they provide (American Psychological Association, 2017b). Therefore, as part of their roles, psychologists should conduct a debrief or referral to the adequate party. In the second ethical conflict, as noted in the second guideline, psychologists should acknowledge the boundaries of the competence (American Psychological Association, 2016b). As explained in the fourth guideline, a psychologist should limit their services only to instances where they have had the adequate formation to execute (American Psychological Association, 2016b).

Summary

In this book, I presented an overview of major roles and responsibilities that forensic practitioners might face in the subspecialties of Civil, Criminal, Juvenile, Police, Correctional, and Investigative forensic psychology. Similarly, I also provided some mitigating factors and potential solutions to address ethical dilemmas and challenges within each discipline. Additionally, I incorporated research that could be relevant to the subspecialties to include controversial issues. It could be concluded that each subspecialty could indeed contribute to the expansion of forensic psychology, psychology in general, and address the specific behavioral needs within a legal setting. Further, it appears that professionals are exposed to multiple challenges that could be addressed with adequate training, experience, ethical code adherence, and proper use of empirical research to engage in informed forensic practice.

Multiple case studies and scenarios were analyzed to explore background, factors, and instruments that assist forensic psychologists in their tasks. Consulting the state laws of Alabama, as well as other states and federal codes assisted this process. Additionally, ethical guidelines were revised and incorporated to address possible practitioner shortcomings pertaining to bias. My intent was to provide a brief overview of the essential topics that surround the interesting forensic psychology field. Hopefully, this overview sparks the curiosity of the reader regarding the commitment that the field of forensic psychology attempts to demonstrate in the legal arena.

References

Ackerman, M. J. (2006). Forensic report writing. *Journal of Clinical Psychology, 62*(1), 59-72. doi:10.1002/jclp.20200

Adebisi, S. S. (2009). Contemporary tools in forensic investigations: The prospects and challenges. *Internet Journal of Forensic Science, 4*(1).

Alabama Code §12-15-203 (2016).

Alabama Criminal Code § 13A-3-1 (2016).

Alabama Criminal Code §13A-5-43.2 (2016).

Allan, A. (2013). Ethics in correctional and forensic psychology: Getting the balance right. *Australian Psychologist, 48*(1), 47-56. doi: 10.1111/j.1742-9544.20 12.00079.x

American Academy of Psychiatry and the Law. (2005). *Ethics guidelines for the practice of forensic psychiatry*. Retrieved from http://www.aapl.org/ethics.htm

American Psychiatric Association. (2013). *Diagnostic and statistical manual of mental disorders* (5th ed.). Arlington, VA: American Psychiatric Publishing.

American Psychological Association. (1990). *Guidelines for providers of psychological services to ethnic, linguistic, and culturally diverse populations*. Retrieved from

http://www.apa.
org/pi/oema/resources/policy/providerguideli
nes.aspx

American Psychological Association (1996). *The
Americans with Disabilities Act and How It
Affects Psychologists.* Retrieved from
http://www.apa.org/pi/disability/resources/p
ub lications/ada.aspx

American Psychological Association. (1993).
Guidelines for providers of psychological
services to ethnic, linguistic, and culturally
diverse populations. *American Psychologist,
48*(1), 45-48. doi: 10.1037/0003-066X.48.1.45

American Psychological Association. (2002).
*Guidelines on multicultural education,
training, research, practice, and
organizational change for psychologists.*
Retrieved from
http://www.apa.org/pi/oema/resources/policy
/multicultur alguidelines.aspx

American Psychological Association.
(2003). Guidelines on multicultural education,
training, research, practice, and organizational
change for Psychologists. *American
Psychologist, 58*(5), 377-402. doi:
10.1037/0003-066X.58.5.377

American Psychological Association.
(2012). Guidelines for assessment of and
intervention with persons with disabilities

American Psychologist, 67(1), 43-62.
doi:10.1037/a0025892

American Psychological Association. (2016a).
Guidelines for child custodyevaluations in family law proceedings. Retrieved fromhttps://www.apa.org/practice/guidelines/child-custody.aspx

American Psychological Association. (2016b).
Specialty Guidelines for Forensic Psychology. Retrieved from http://www.apa.org/practice/guidelines/forensic-psychology.aspx

American Psychological Association. (2017a). *APA Warns Against Reinstituting 'Enhanced' Interrogation.* Retrieved from http://www.apa.org/news/press/releases/2017/01/reinstitutinginterrogation.aspx

American Psychological Association. (2017b). *Ethical Principles of Psychologists and Code of Conduct with 2010 and 2016 Amendments.* Retrieved from http://www.apa.org/ethics/code/index.aspx

American Psychology-Law Society. (2016).
Conferences. Retrieved from http://apls.wildapricot.org/resources/Documents/APLS2016/2016ConferenceProgram.pdf

Andrés-Pueyo, A., & Echeburúa, E. (2010). Valoración del riesgo de violencia: Instrumentos disponibles e indicaciones de aplicación. =

Violence risk assessment: Available tools and instructions for use. *Psicothema, 22*(3), 403-409.

Arbach, K., Bondaruk, A., Carubelli, S., Palma Vegar, M. F., & Singh, J. P. (2017). Evaluación forense de la peligrosidad: Una aproximación a las prácticas profesionales en Latinoamérica. *Psiencia: Revista Latinoamericana De Ciencia Psicológica, 9*(1), 1-15. doi: 10.5872/psiencia/9.1.23

Babitsky, S., Mangraviti, J. J. (Producers). (2000). *Cross-examination: How to be an effective and ethical expert witness,* Falmouth, MA: Seak, Inc.

Bartol, C. R., & Bartol, A. M. (2012). *Introduction to forensic psychology: research and application* (4th ed.) Thousand Oaks, CA: Sage Publications, Inc.

Boccaccini, M. T. (2002). What do we really know about witness preparation? *Behavioral Sciences and the Law, 20*(1), 161–189. doi:10.1002/bsl.472

Bonnie, R. J., & Slobogin, C. (1980). The role of mental health professionals in the criminal process: The case for informed speculation. *Virginia Law Review, 66*(3), 427–522.

Brodsky, S. L. (2004). *Coping with cross-examination and other pathways to effective testimony*. Washington, DC: American Psychological Association.

Brodsky, S. L. (2007). Correctional psychology and the American Association of Correctional Psychology: A revisionist history. *Criminal Justice and Behavior, 34*(6), 862–869. doi: 10.1177/0093854807301993

Burks v. State, 600 Ala. 374 (1991).

Butcher, J. N., Graham, J. R., BenPorath, Y. S., Tellegen, A., Dahlstrom, W. G., & Kaemmer, B. (2001). *MMPI–2 (Minnesota multiphasic personality inventory 2) Manual for administration, scoring, and interpretation* (Revised ed.). Minneapolis, MN: University of Minnesota Press.

Calamari Productions (Producer). (2012). *Young kids, hard time director's cut* [Video file]. Retrieved from https://www.youtube.com/watch?v=g3lw6PMjj40

Canter, D., & Youngs, D. (2012). Narratives of criminal action and forensic psychology. *Legal and Criminological Psychology, 17*(2), 262-275. doi: 10.111 1/j.2044-8333.2012.02050.x

Carmichael, J. T., & Burgos, G. (2012). Sentencing juvenile offenders to life in prison: The political sociology of juvenile punishment. *American Journal of Criminal Justice, 37*(4), 602-629. doi: 10.1007/s12103-011-9135-1

Christie, R. (1976). Probability v. precedence: The social psychology of jury selection. In G.Bermant, C.Nemeth, & N.Vidmar (Eds.*),* *Psychology and the law* (pp. 265–281). Lexington: Lexington Books.

Civil Rights Act of 1964 § 7, 42 U.S.C. § 2000 et seq (1964).

Cox, M. L., & Zapf, P. A. (2004). An investigation of discrepancies between mental health professionals and the courts in decisions about competency. *Law & Psychology Review, 28,* 109-132. Retrieved from

Daubert v. Merrell Dow Pharmaceuticals, 509 U.S. 579 (1993).

Day, A., & Casey, S. (2009). Values in forensic and correctional psychology. *Aggression and Violent Behavior*, *14*(4), 232-238. doi: 10.1016/j.avb.2009.03.008

deRuiter, C., & Kaser-Boyd, N. (2015). *Forensic psychological assessment inpractice: Case studies*. New York, NY: Routledge.

Death Penalty Information Center. (2017). *Facts about the Death Penalty*. Retrieved from https://deathpenaltyinfo.org/documents/Fact Sheet.pdf

Determination of mental competency to stand trial to undergo post-release proceedings, 18 U.S.C. § 4241 (2012).

Dusky v. U.S., 362 US 402 (1960).

Edkins, V. A., Falligant, J. M., Lavoie, J., & Lawal, T. (2017). Psychology and the legal system: The courtroom and beyond. *Translational Issues in Psychological Science, 3*(2), 117-120. doi: 10.1037/tps0000119

FindLaw. (2013). *Rights of Inmates.* Retrieved from http://civilrights.findlaw.com/other-constitutional-rights/rights-ofinmates.html

Flynn, A. (2000). Procedural default: A de facto exception to civility? *Capital Defense Journal, 12*(2), 289–304.

Franklin, D. J. (2011a). *Competency Evaluations-Wills and Guardianships.* Retrieved from http://psychologyinfo.com/forensic/competency.html

Franklin, D. J. (2011b). *Forensic Psychology-Civil Court.* Retrieved from http://psychologyinfo.com/forensic/civil_court.html

Franklin, D. J. (2011c). *Forensic Psychology-Family Court.* Retrieved from http://psycholog yinfo.com/forensic/child_custody.html

Franklin, D. J. (2011d). *Personal Injury Evaluations.* Retrieved from http://psycholo gyinfo.com/forensic/personal_injury.html

Franklin, D. J. (2011e). *Psychological Factors in Sexual Harassment.*Retrieved from http://psychologyinfo.com/forensic/harassme nt.html

Geneva Convention Relative to the Protection of Civilian Persons in Time of War. Oct. 21, 1950. 75 U.N.T.S. 287. Retrieved from http://www.ohchr.org/EN/Pr ofessionalInterest/Pages/TreatmentOfPrisoner sOfWar.aspx

Gianvanni, E., & Sharman, S. J. (2017). Legal Representatives' Opinions regarding Psychologists Engaging in Expert Witness Services in Australian Courts and Tribunals. *Psychiatry, Psychology & Law*, *24*(2), 223-232. doi: 10.1080/13 218719.2016.1254589

Giorgi-Guarnieri, D., Janofsky, J., Keram, E., Lawsky, S., Merideth, P., Mossman, D., Schwart-Watts, D., Scott, C., Thompson, J. Jr., & Zonana, H. (2002). AAPL practice guideline for forensic psychiatric evaluation of defendants raising the insanity defense. *Journal of the American Academy of Psychiatry and Law*, *30*(2), S3– 40.

González-Sala, F., Osca-Lluch, J., Gil, F. T., & Ortega, M. P. (2017). Characterization of Legal Psychology through psychology journals included in Criminology & Penology and Law categories of Web of Science. *Anales de Psicología*, *33*(2), 411-416. doi: 10.6018/analesps.33.2.262591

Goodman, J. (2012). Crime and socioeconomic conditions: Evidence for non-cultural domain specificity in evolutionary forensic psychology. *Aggression and Violent Behavior, 17*(6), 523-526. doi: 10.1016/j.avb.2012.07.007

Gottlieb, M. C., & Coleman, A. (2012). Ethical challenges in forensic psychology practice. In S. J. Knapp, M. C. Gottlieb, M. M. Handelsman, L. D. VandeCreek, S. J. Knapp, M. C. Gottlieb, L. D. VandeCreek (Eds.), *APA handbook of ethics in psychology, Vol 2: Practice, teaching, and research* (pp. 91-123). Washington, DC, US: American Psychological Association. doi:10.1037/13272-006

Gowensmith, W. N., Murrie, D. C., Boccaccini, M. T., & McNichols, B. J. (2017). Field reliability influences field validity: Risk assessments of individuals found not guilty by reason of insanity. *Psychological Assessment, 29*(6), 786-794. doi:10.1037/pas0000376

Greene, E., & Evelo, A. J. (2013). Attitudes regarding life sentences for juvenile offenders. *Law and Human Behavior, 37*(4), 276–289. doi: 10.1037/lhb0000031

Guarnera, L. A., Murrie, D. C., & Boccaccini, M. T. (2017). Why do forensic experts disagree? Sources of unreliability and bias in forensic psychology evaluations. *Translational Issues in Psychological Science, 3*(2), 143-152. doi: 10.1037/tps0000114

Haney, C. (1993). Psychology and legal change: The impact of a decade. *Law and Human Behavior*, *17*(4), 371–398. doi: 10.1007/BF01044374

Hare, R. D. (2016). Psychopathy, the PCL-R, and criminal justice: Some new findings and current issues. *Canadian Psychology/PsychologieCanadienne*, *57*(1), 21–34. doi: 10.1037/cap0000041

Harvey, V. S. (2006). Variables affecting the clarity of psychological reports. *Journal of Clinical Psychology*, *62*(1), 5-18. doi:10.1002/jclp.20196

Haun, J. J., Gallagher, J. A., & Milz, A. A. (2010). The Influence of Time and Treatment on Recall of Mental State at the Time of Offense: Incompetent Defendants and Evaluation of Insanity. *Journal of Forensic Psychology Practice*, *10*(5), 464-475. doi: 10.1080/15228932.2010.489868

Hibler, N.S. (2002). An Interesting Career in Psychology: Police Psychology in the Federal Government. *Psychological Science Agenda, 15*(5).

Huss, M. T. (2001). What is forensic psychology? It's not silence of the lambs. *Eye on Psi Chi*. Retrieved from http://www.psichi.org/?page=053EyeSpring01cHuss

Hutson, M. (2007). Unnatural selection. *Psychology Today.* Retrieved from http://www.psychologytoday.com/articles/20 0703/unnaturalselection

Iacono, W. G. (2008). The forensic application of "brain fingerprinting": Why scientists should encourage the use of P300 memory detection methods. *American Journal of Bioethics, 8*(1), 30–32. doi: 10.1080/15265160701828550

International Association for Correctional and Forensic Psychology. (2010). Standards for Psychology Services in Jails, Prisons, Correctional Facilities, and Agencies. *Criminal Justice and Behavior, 37*(7), 749–808. doi: 10.1177/0093854810368253

Kalis, A., & Meynen, G. (2014). Mental disorder and legal responsibility: The relevance of stages of decision making. *International Journal of Law and Psychiatry, 37*(6), 601-608. doi:10.1016/j.ijlp.2014.02.034

Kanemoto, C. S. (2005). Bushido in the courtroom: A case for virtue orientedlawyering. *South Carolina Law Review, 57*, 357–386.

Kassin, S. M., Appleby, S. C., & TorkildsonPerillo, J. (2010). Interviewing suspects: Practice, science, and future directions. *Legal and Criminal Psychology, 15*(1), 39–55. doi: 10.1348/135532509X449361

Killing persons aiding Federal investigations or State correctional officers. 8 U.S.C. of 1994 § 1121 (1996).

Knox, D., Limbacher, J., & McMahan, K. (1993). Thomas Dillon, hunter of humans. *Akron Beacon Journal*. Retrieved from http://www.freerepublic.com/focus/news/767482/posts

Kolivoski, K. M., & Shook, J. J. (2016). Incarcerating juveniles in adult prisons: Examining the relationship between age and prison behavior in transferred juveniles. *Criminal Justice and Behavior, 43*(9), 1242-1259. doi: 10.1177/0093854816631793

Le Goff, C., Poncet, D., & Jeanneau, Y. (Producers). (2001). *Murder on a Sunday morning*. France & U.S.: Docurama.

Lieberman, J. D. & Sales, B. D. (2006). *Scientific Jury Selection*. Washington, D.C.: American Psychological Association.

Littlefield, M. (2009). Constructing the organ of deceit: The rhetoric of fMRI and brain fingerprinting in post 9/11 America.*Science, Technology, & Human Values, 34*(3) 365–392. doi: 10.1177/0162243908328756

Louden, J. E., & Skeem, J. L. (2007). Constructing insanity: Jurors' prototypes, attitudes, and legal decision-making. *Behavioral Sciences & the Law*, 25(4), 449-470. doi:10.1002/bsl.760

Mark, M. M. (1999). Social science evidence in the courtroom: Daubert and beyond? Psychology, *Public Policy, and Law, 5*(1), 175–193. doi:10.1037//1076-

McKee, G. R. (n.d.). *Forensic psychology consultation in criminal cases*. Retrieved from http://expertpages.com/news/mckee.htm

McLaughlin, J. L., & Kan, L. Y. (2014). Test usage in four common types of forensic mental health assessment. *Professional Psychology: Research and Practice, 45*(2), 128–135. doi: 10.1037/a0036318

McLellan, F. (2006). Mental health and justice: the case of Andrea Yates. *Lancet (London, England), 368*(9551), 1951-1954. doi: 10.1016/S0140-6736(06)69789-4

Means, R. F., Heller, L. D., & Janofsky, J. S. (2012). Transferring juvenile defendants from adult to juvenile court: How Maryland forensic evaluators and judges reach their decisions. *Journal of The American Academy of Psychiatry and The Law, 40*(3), 333-340. Retrieved from https://www.ncbi.nlm.nih.gov/pubmed/22960915

Melton, G. B., Petrila, J., Poythress, N. G., & Slobogin, C. (2007). *Psychological evaluations for the courts: A handbook for mental health professionals and lawyers* (3rd ed.). New York: The Guilford Press.

Meritor Savings Bank v. Vinson, 477 U.S. 57 (1986).
Miller, T. W., Clark, J., Veltkamp, L. J., Burton, D. C., & Swope, M. (2008). Teleconferencing model for forensic consultation, court testimony, and continuing education. *Behavioral Sciences & the Law*, 26(3), 301–313. doi: 10.1002/bsl.809

Moses, R. (2001). *Misidentification: The caprices of eyewitness testimony in criminal cases*. Retrieved from http://criminaldefense.homestead. com/eyewitnessmisidentification.html

Motor vehicles. 18 U.S.C. of 1992 § 2119 (1996).

Nagin, D. (2014). Deterrence and the death penalty: Why the statistics should be ignored. *Significance, 11*(2), 9–13. doi: 10.1111/j.17409713.2014 .00733.x

National Conference of State Legislatures. (n.d.). *Adolescent development and competency: Juvenile justice guidebook for legislators*. Retrieved from http://www.ncsl.org/document s/cj/jjguidebook-adolescent.pdf

Nichols, D. S. (2011*). Essentials of MMPI2assessment* (2nd ed.). New York: John Wiley & Sons, Inc.

Ortiz-Díaz, S. M. (2018). *The impacts of religious discrimination towards anxiety in diverse populations* (Order No. 10687721). Available from ProQuest Dissertations & Theses Global. (1981955188). Retrieved from

http://ezp.waldenulibrary.org
/login?url=https://search-proquest
com.ezp.waldenulibrary.org/docvie
w/1981955188?accountid=14872

Otto, R. K., & Heilburn, K. (2002). The practice of
forensic psychology: A look toward the future
in light of the past. *American Psychologist,
57*(1), 5–18. doi: 10.1037/0003-066X.57.1.5

Patel, S., & Choate, L. (2014). Conducting child
custody evaluations: Best practices for mental
health counselors who are court-appointed as
child custody evaluators. *Journal of Mental
Health Counseling*, 36(1), 18–30. doi:
10.17744/mehc.36.1.e00401wv7134w505

People v. Goldstein. 4 A.D.3d 32 (2004).

People v. Goldstein. N.Y. 1 No. 155 (2005).

People v. Gonzáles, 430 U.S. 655 (1980).

Perillo, J. T., & Kassin, S. M. (2011). Inside
interrogation: The lie, the bluff, and false
confessions. *Law and Human Behavior, 35*(4),
327–337. doi: 10.1007/s10979-01

Perri, F. S., & Lichtenwald, T. G. (2009). When worlds
collide: Criminal investigative analysis, forensic
psychology, and the Timothy Masters case. *The
Forensic Examiner*, *18*(2), 52-68.

Pirelli, G., Zapf, P. A. & Gottdiener, W. H. (2011). A
Meta-Analytic Review of Competency to Stand

Trial Research. *Psychology, Public Policy, and Law, 17*(1), 1-53. doi: 10.1037/a0021713

Pittel, S. M., Bloom, B., & SIlen, P. (n.d.). *Jury selection—asking the right questions: A way to improve the art of jury selection.* Retrieved from http://www.allaboutforensicpsychology.com/juryselection.html

Poythress, N. (1980). Coping on the witness stand: Learned responses to "learned treatises." *Professional Psychology, 11*(1), 139–149. doi:10.1037/0735-7028.11.1.139

Reich, W. A. (2014). Mental health screening outcomes among justice-involved youths under community supervision. *Journal of Offender Rehabilitation, 53*(3), 211-230. doi:10.1080/10509674.2014.887607

Resendes, J., & Lecci, L. (2012). Comparing the MMPI-2 scale scores of parents involved in parental competency and child custody assessments. *Psychological Assessment, 24*(4), 1054–1059. doi: 10.1037/a0028585

Rohde, D. (1999, October 23). Expert Disputes Schizophrenia Defense. *New York Times.* p. B3.

Rules of Evidence of 1975, 28 U.S.C. § 2072 (2014).

Shaw, J., Öhman, L., & van Koppen, P. (2013). Psychology and law: The past, present, and future of the discipline. *Psychology, Crime & Law*, *19*(8), 643-647. doi: 10.1080/1068316X.2013.793979

Shepherd, S. M., & Lewis-Fernández, R. (2016). Forensic risk assessment and cultural diversity: Contemporary challenges and future directions. *Psychology, Public Policy, and Law*, *22*(4), 427-438. doi:10.1037/law0000102

Shuman, D. W., & Sales, B. D. (1999). The impact of *Daubert*and its progeny on the admissibility of behavioral and social science evidence. *Psychology, Public Policy, and Law*, *5*(1), 3–15. doi:10.1037/1076-8971.5.1.3

Shuman, D. W., Cunningham, M. D., Connell, M. A., & Reid, W. H. (2003). Interstate forensic psychology consultations: A call for reform and proposal of a model rule. *Professional Psychology: Research and Practice*, *34*(3), 233-239. doi:10.1037/0735-7028.34.3.233

Storey, J. E., Hart, S. D., Cooke, D. J., & Michie, C. (2016). Psychometric properties of the Hare Psychopathy Checklist-Revised (PCL-R) in a representative sample of Canadian federal offenders. *Law and Human Behavior, 40*(2), 136–146. doi: 10.1037/lhb0000174

Sweet, D. M., Meissner, C. A., & Atkinson, D. J. (2017). Assessing Law Enforcement Performance in Behavior-Based Threat Detection Tasks Involving a Concealed Weapon or Device. *Law and Human Behavior,*doi: 10.1037/lhb0000243

Taylor v. State. 10 Ala. 1037 (2004).

The John D. and Catherine T. MacArthur Foundation. (2006). *MacArthur Foundation Research Network on Adolescent Development and Juvenile Justice.* Retrieved from http://www.adj j.org/downlo ads/552network_overview.pdf

Torrie, J. (Writer) & Author (Director). (2014). *The psychopath next door* [Television series episode]. In Author (Producer), *Doc Zone.* Kelowna, BC: High Definition Pictures.

U.S. Const. amend. V.

U.S. Department of Justice. (2006). *Society for Military Psychology: Strategic Plan 2007– 2012: Charting a Course for the Future.* Retrieved from http://www.justi ce.gov/archive/mps/strategic2007- 2012/strategic_plan20072012.pdf

U.S. Equal Employment Opportunity Commission (2017). *Americans with Disabilities Act Questions and Answers.* Retrieved from https://www.ada.gov/archive/q & aeng02.htm

Uniform Code of Military Justice. (1950). 10 U.S.C. § 802 § 2.

van Wijk, A., Loeber, R., Vermeiren, R., Pardini, D., Bullens, R., & Doreleijers, T. (2005). Violent juvenile sex offenders compared with violent juvenile nonsex offenders: explorative findings from the Pittsburgh Youth Study. *Sexual Abuse: A Journal of Research & Treatment, 17*(3), 333-352. doi: 10.1007/s11194-005-5062-3

Varela, J. G., & Conroy, M. A. (2012). Professional competencies in forensic psychology. *Professional Psychology: Research and Practice, 43*(5), 410–421. doi: 10.1037/a0026776

Vitacco, M. J., Erickson, S. K., Kurus, S., & Apple, B. N. (2012). The role of the Violence Risk Appraisal Guide and Historical, Clinical, Risk-20 in U.S. courts: A case law survey. *Psychology, Public Policy, and Law, 18*(3), 361–391. doi: 10.1037/a0025834

Vogel, B. L., & Vogel, R. E. (2003). The age of death: appraising public opinion of juvenile capital punishment. *Journal of Criminal Justice, 31*(2). 169-183. doi: 10.1016/S0047-2352(02)00223-4

Wadsworth Cengage Learning. (2007). *Writing and communicating for criminal justice*. Belmont, CA: Author.

Weiner, I. B., & Otto, R. K. (2013). *The handbook of forensic psychology* (4th ed.). New York, NY: Wiley.

West, D. A., & Lichtenstein, B. (2006). Andrea Yates and the Criminalization of the Filicidal Maternal Body. *Feminist Criminology, 1*(3), 173-187. doi: 10.1177/1557085106288863

Winslow, F. (1854). Lecture III. On medico-legal evidence in cases of insanity. In,*Lettsomian on insanity* (pp. 82-160). London, Great Britain: John Churchill. doi:10.1037/12106-003

Wormith, J. S., Althouse, R., Simpson, M., Reitzel, L., Fagan, T., & Morgan, R. (2007). The rehabilitation and reintegration of offenders: The current landscape and some future directions for correctional psychology. *Criminal Justice and Behavior, 34*(7), 879–892. doi: 10.1177/0093854807301552

Yakush, B. A., & Wolbransky, M. (2013). Insanity and the definition of wrongfulness in California. *Journal of Forensic Psychology Practice*, *13*(4), 355-372. doi:10.1080 b/15228932.2013.820992

Yates v. State, 171 U.S. 215 (2005).

Zapf, P. A., Boccaccini, M. T., & Brodsky, S. L. (2003). Assessment of competency for execution: professional guidelines and an evaluation checklist. *Behavioral Sciences & The Law*, *21*(1), 103-120. doi:10.1002/bsl.491

Zimring, F. E., Jennings, W. G., Piquero, A. R., & Hays, S. (2009). Investigating the continuity of sex offending: Evidence from the second

Philadelphia birth cohort.*Justice Quarterly, 26*, 58-76. doi: 10.1080/07418820801989734

Zumbach, J., & Koglin, U. (2015). Psychological evaluations in family law proceedings: A systematic review of the contemporary literature. *Professional Psychology: Research and Practice, 46*(4), 221–234. doi: 10.1037/a0039329

Zur, O., & González, S. (2002). *Multiple Relationships in Military Psychology*. Retrieved from http://www.zurinstitute.com/dualmilitary.html

About the Author

Sharlaine Ortiz has formally studied psychology and human behavior since 2006. While completing her doctorate in clinical psychology, Sharlaine specialized in forensic psychology for its application on the legal system in criminal and civil courts. As a combat veteran, Sharlaine provided analysis of information on internal and external threats and political, legal, and military aspects of events to mitigate hostile behavior. While overseas, Sharlaine worked as a subject matter expert for the Department of Defense regarding threat and risk assessment for civil, military, governmental, and law enforcement organizations. Sharlaine is a member of the International Honor Society of Psychology Psi Chi and former secretary of one of the first Psi Chi chapters ever established in the Caribbean. She is also a member of the Golden Key International Honor Society.

HowExpert publishes quick 'how to' guides on all topics from A to Z by everyday experts. Visit HowExpert.com to learn more.

Recommended Resources

- HowExpert.com – Quick 'How To' Guides on All Topics by Everyday Experts.
- HowExpert.com/books – HowExpert Books
- HowExpert.com/products – HowExpert Products
- HowExpert.com/courses – HowExpert Courses
- HowExpert.com/clothing – HowExpert Clothing
- HowExpert.com/membership – Learn All Topics from A to Z by Real Experts.
- HowExpert.com/affiliates – HowExpert Affiliate Program
- HowExpert.com/jobs – HowExpert Jobs
- HowExpert.com/writers – Write About Your #1 Passion/Knowledge/Expertise.
- YouTube.com/HowExpert – Subscribe to HowExpert YouTube.
- Instagram.com/HowExpert – Follow HowExpert on Instagram.
- Facebook.com/HowExpert – Follow HowExpert on Facebook.